NAUGHTY SECRETS

NAUGHTY SECRETS

What Your Neighbors Are *Really* Doing Behind Their Bedroom Doors!

JOAN ELIZABETH LLOYD

WARNER BOOKS

An AOL Time Warner Company

Copyright © 2003 by Joan Elizabeth Lloyd
All rights reserved.

Warner Books, Inc., 1271 Avenue of the Americas, New York, NY 10020

 An AOL Time Warner Company

Printed in the United States of America

ISBN 0-7394-3225-7

Book design and text composition by Nancy Sabato
Cover design by Janet Perr
Cover photo by IPS / Photonica

This book is dedicated to all of the wonderful people who spent their time filling out my questionnaire. I can't thank them enough for all their hard work. I hope they enjoyed the effort, learned something about themselves and their sex lives, and maybe even found the courage to share some of it with their partner. Sex can get better and better as the years pass. Ed and I are living proof.

CONTENTS

A BRIEF INTRODUCTION

ABOUT THE
SURVEY AND THE
RESPONDENTS

Ever wanted to peek into your neighbors' bedrooms? I think we're all curious to see what "real people" do, how they make love. What games do they play? What toys do they play with? What fantasies do they have? Do they act them out?

Why do we want to know? Maybe for ideas—*What are they doing that my partner and I can incorporate into our sex lives?* Maybe out of curiosity—*Mary and John always look so content. I wonder what they're doing that leads them to grin at each other "that way."* Maybe to see whether we are unusual in what *we* do behind closed doors—*Does anyone else enjoy being blindfolded? Playing doctor?*

For many years I've been writing books on sex and relationships and running a Web site at JoanELloyd.com devoted to the frank interchange of ideas. Well, I finally got curious, too. So my last book, *Totally Private,* included a survey to see what "normal folks" were doing and how they were feeling.

I can hear you now—*Normal folks? What the heck does that mean?* Over the years I've been asked the same questions over and over again. One of the most common questions, although phrased differently in each letter, boils down to *Am I normal?* Well, let's answer that once and for all. Here are ordinary men and women discussing what they do in the privacy of their bedroom.

When I first published the survey, both in *Totally Private* and on my Web site, I expected to get responses. I told myself that this was a totally unscientific survey since only a few brave souls would have the honesty and time to respond. Well, I still don't see anything scientific about it, because the folks who filled out the survey had bought a book about sex or visited my sexually oriented Web site, but the number of responses floored me. Hundreds of people took their valuable time to fill out a survey and send it to me. Bravo to all of them, and I thank them all so much. These aren't *my* neighbors, you say. Maybe that's true, but they are someone's neighbors.

Several people told me that they had copied the survey, keeping one copy and giving another to their partner. They each worked in private, then exchanged their answers as a step toward more open communication. Others found that filling out the survey helped them learn what had slipped away over the years that might be recaptured. If you're interested in filling out the survey, for any of the above reasons or just for kicks and giggles, one is included at the end of this book.

This book is filled with real letters from real people. Do they make love the same way you do? Some do, but many don't. You'll find some of their answers off-putting—*No way I'd ever be interested in doing what that person did.* But still . . . some of the answers will intrigue you. *Hmm. I never thought of that. I'd kinda like to try it.* Great; that's part of the reason I wrote the book. But how do you discuss something new and maybe a bit unusual with your partner?

In my first book, *Nice Couples Do,* I introduced a technique called Bookmarking, and it will work wonderfully with *Naughty Secrets* as well. If you find an idea anywhere in the book that curls your toes, slip a bookmark in that page and give the book to your partner. Then leave him or her alone to read and react in private.

One of two things can happen. One: He or she may be titillated by the idea. Fabulous! You two have begun a communication that can make your desire come true.

The other: He or she may not be turned on by the activity you've marked. That's fine, too. Hopefully he or she will realize the risk you've taken by placing the bookmark in the first place. You've risked your partner's censure in order to improve your sex life. Bravo! So, partner, take the same risk. Move the bookmark to something that lights your own fire instead, then return the book. That way you two have begun a dialogue that can lead to some very interesting exchanges and some spicier sex.

Okay, let's get down to the nitty-gritty. Who answered the survey? Almost exactly half of those who responded were men, and they ranged in age from twenty-one to seventy-eight. The women ranged from nineteen to sixty-two. About half were permanently partnered.

I asked folks to respond with straight or gay, and I do apologize for limiting answers that way. I was taken to task by a few people who said they were bisexual. Thanks for setting me straight. I truly believe that heterosexuality is at one end of a continuum and homosexuality at the other. Many people fall somewhere in between, primarily straight but enjoying an occasional same-sex relationship or primarily gay with some heterosexual relationships as well. So where it's relevant to the answer, I've noted their bisexuality. Sadly, I didn't get any responses from anyone who identified him- or herself as a homosexual.

Are all the stories they told me true? Who knows? Some of them might be touched with a bit of wishful thinking, but let's just take everyone at their word. Also, lots of people used explicit language. I didn't want to change too much and spoil the sense of what they wrote. Occasionally I softened the words a bit and edited the contents, but most of the stories are as the writers penned them.

One last note. No idea is included in only one section. Some of the best sex ever involved fantasies, oral or anal sex, as did some of the worst, the most unusual . . . well, you get the idea. So skip around and merely ignore letters and/or sections that don't interest you. Play and have some fun.

Okay, let's get to it. How do those who filled out the survey think about sex, about their partner, about themselves? Let's learn all their Naughty Secrets.

one

YOUR NEIGHBORS' SEX LIFE

The First Time, the Best, the Worst,
the Most Embarrassing, the Most Wonderful

TELL ME ABOUT
THE FIRST TIME
YOU MADE LOVE

Ever wonder whether your neighbors' first times were similar to yours? Or whether they matched those romantic encounters in romance novels? You know the ones—he knows just what to do and she experiences a small stab of pain followed by an intense orgasm. Then they fall in love and she vows never to forget that wonderful night they spent together. Oh, and she's not left with any mess.

Well, I can tell you mine didn't. As a matter of fact, I don't actually remember my first time. My then-boyfriend—later husband and ex-husband—and I petted and approached actual intercourse more and more closely with each encounter. Although I don't remember the specific evening, we eventually just did it. It obviously didn't feel like crossing any big hurdle, since that particular evening, probably spent in the front seat of a 1954 Ford, doesn't stand out in my mind. As for the quick stab of pain, I assume my membrane was torn long before that night from bike riding, or roller skating and falling, or just from general wear and tear. For whatever reason, I had neither hymen nor pain.

But that's just me. Let's peek in on the neighbors and see what their first times were like. Surprisingly, a lot of people couldn't remember what their first time was like, either, and a lot of people who responded didn't think their first time was a big deal at all.

A twenty-two-year-old woman wrote:

I don't really remember it, which is odd because it wasn't even four years ago. It was planned out. We had talked and he had bought condoms. We ended up not waiting until "the night," which was a good thing because I got my period that day. I do remember it didn't hurt like I thought it would, but it wasn't exactly ecstasy either.

A thirty-year-old woman wrote:

To be honest with you I don't remember my first time. It was in my early twenties, I think, but I don't recall the details.

A forty-one-year-old woman wrote:

My parents were out of town and I had pretty much decided I wanted to lose my virginity soon. I was sixteen and a younger girlfriend and I had made our way to a nearby town for the evening. We met up with a couple of guys she knew and they took us to a basement apartment. My friend left with one of the guys and I found myself alone with the other fellow, whom I didn't even know. We started making out and I let him go all the way. It was a little painful but a bit stimulating, too, although I didn't have an orgasm. I got up and left after he fell asleep.

A forty-seven-year-old woman wrote:

He just did it. It didn't really hurt, it was just boring.

A forty-one-year-old man wrote:

All I can remember is that I was really scared.

A twenty-five-year-old woman wrote:

The fist time I had sex I was in the eighth grade and the guy was in high school. We'd planned the night for a week and I'd man-

aged to get my parents out of the house for a few hours. His penis was small and he didn't play with me or anything. I didn't
really feel much: no pain or pleasure. I had been so anxious to finally have sex only to be completely disappointed.

A thirty-four-year-old woman wrote:

My first time was nothing spectacular. It wasn't fun, wasn't bad,
didn't hurt, and needless to say I didn't orgasm. It was very much
a disappointment. I remember thinking, *Is this what all the fuss is
about?*

A thirty-year-old man wrote:

It happened on the beach in North Carolina when I was fourteen. We had a clumsy, disastrous screw in an abandoned
house. All I can say for the experience is that I lost my virginity.
That's about it.

A twenty-two-year-old man wrote:

I was nineteen and, although I had been trying to get laid for
years, I was still a virgin. I hadn't done anything past kissing, and
felt really left out.

I met this girl who was very experienced and, after going out
for a few weeks, we decided to give it a try. She just lay there and
let me do everything, which, for a very inexperienced young
man, was a bit daunting.

It was not what I'd expected at all. It felt like masturbating inside someone, not sex. I eventually realized that was how she
liked sex: me doing everything while she just lay there. We broke
up a year or so later after quite a boring sex life.

A forty-five-year-old man wrote:

I had been dating a girl in a college class with me for a few
weeks, and we were at her apartment having some wine and
cheese with crackers, just talking. One thing led to another, and
we ended up in bed.

I wasn't trying to get laid, but when she took her clothes off and then undressed me, well, I thought, here I go! Unfortunately the wine didn't help me when it came to trying to delay my orgasm so I came almost immediately. I pretended that nothing had happened and continued to stroke her even though I just felt like lying still. Soon my erection faded, and I fell out. I admitted to her that I couldn't hold out. I'm sure it was not a memorable fuck for her.

A *fifty-four-year-old man wrote:*

My first time was with a prostitute when I was eighteen and drunk. It was sex but not all that rewarding.

A *twenty-five-year-old woman wrote:*

My first time was several years back when my then-boyfriend reserved a hotel room. We got to the room, and we just lay on the bed kissing and caressing.

I wasn't too sure that I actually wanted to go all the way, but as things got hotter I couldn't resist. It wasn't quite what I expected, mainly because he kept missing my opening and pushing in the wrong areas. Granted, I wasn't 100 percent sure what to do, either, but I knew it felt wrong.

He finally found the right spot, and once he was inside I liked the feeling of it. It didn't hurt like I thought it might and I didn't scream out in pain like people had said I would.

After it was over, however, I thought, *Is that it? That wasn't as amazing as people said it should be.* I worried that there was something wrong with me, but now I know better.

A *thirty-one-year-old man wrote:*

My first time was as a sophomore in high school with a freshman girl whom I had been dating for about six months. We were at her house while her parents were out of town, drinking some of their wine. It was what I consider the typical bumbling attempt at intimacy that most teenagers call sex.

These next answers are from folks who found their first experience really awful.

A twenty-two-year-old woman wrote:

I was with a complete jerk who was more worried about getting his rocks off than being easy with me. He sat me on top of him, placed his arms under mine with his hands on my shoulders and jerked me down, forcing his penis into me. I bled for a week.

A fifty-six-year-old man wrote:

My first time for intercourse was with my first wife, and it was so bad that it probably was an indication of why we should never have gotten married!

A twenty-three-year-old woman wrote:

My first time was with a guy whom I had dated for a few months and I think I did it just to do it. I had no idea what an orgasm was or that it could be pleasing. In fact I cried because it hurt, and went home feeling dirty and ashamed. I remember thinking that I was never going to do it again. I couldn't believe that people do such crazy things for sex, because it really wasn't all it was cracked up to be.

A twenty-six-year-old woman wrote:

It was horrible. After he was done he got up, pulled up his pants, looked at me, and left. He told all of our friends that "we had sex" but never spoke to me again.

A seventy-seven-year-old man wrote:

My first time was while I was in the army in World War II. It was an older woman, a prostitute. Although she was kind and tried everything, I never came. It took me a long time to recover from that.

A thirty-two-year-old woman wrote:

Basically the guy was a jerk who tried to get me drunk at a college frat party many years ago. We kissed, he grabbed my tits a couple of times, then went straight for my crotch. He rubbed it for a minute, took me to his room. I was young and stupid and I just lay there while he did his thing.

A *fifty-five-year-old man* wrote:

It was a true disaster. The girl was six or seven years older than I was, and she found out that I was a nineteen-year-old virgin. Alter pulling me into her bedroom, we started kissing and groping each other. It took about forty-five seconds of her hand for me to cover her with my come. How embarrassing!

A *thirty-three-year-old woman* wrote:

It sucked. It was with my ex-husband who was my boyfriend at the time. Wham, bam, and then he said he couldn't wait to tell his friends. As I look back on it, I wonder now why I married him at all.

A *forty-three-year-old woman* wrote:

The only reason I did it was because my sister, who was younger than I was, had been doing the deed for a while. At the time I was almost nineteen and I guess I let my boyfriend talk me into it.

After I had my clothes off, I chickened out and told him I did not want to do it. He would not let me stop and forced me to do it anyway. No amount of crying or begging made him listen. To make matters worse, my sister was in the next room and heard me crying and pleading with him to stop. She couldn't do anything about it. To me sex sucked and I saw no future in it.

A *fifty-year-old woman* wrote:

It was painful, I was afraid, and I hated it. I did it that once and didn't do it again for two years.

A thirty-year-old woman wrote:

My first time was with this guy I really liked. He pressured me into it, telling me he'd love me more if we did it. I guess I fell for that, so we went to his house and had sex on his bedroom floor. Not only did it hurt but I bled a lot. He never talked to me again.

A fifty-six-year-old man wrote:

My first time, and hers, was on our honeymoon. We got all hot and I pushed my cock into her. As hard as I tried, I couldn't get all the way in. Frustrated, we tried again later and the same thing happened, and continued happening all that week.

When we returned she went to the doctor and it turned out that her hymen was very thick and it had to be surgically broken. Once it was, and she waited as long as the doctor said, we finally did it. Maybe because we had had to wait too long, it was explosive for both of us.

A nineteen-year-old woman wrote:

My first time was really bad for several reasons. First of all, I was too young, only fifteen at the time. Second, we were both virgins and very stupid about sex. We lasted maybe a minute before we both got scared and stopped. Then, until I got my period three weeks later, we were scared to death I was pregnant, even though we used a condom and he never got off. See how stupid we were?

Of course, some lucky folks really enjoyed their first time.

A twenty-seven-year-old woman wrote:

It was a very good experience, with a guy I really cared about. He spent a lot of time making sure it was great for me, exciting me orally and making me come that way before he even tried to enter me.

A *twenty-five-year-old man* wrote:

I was quite young, maybe fifteen or sixteen, and my friend's mother seduced me.

My friend had left me at his house and had gone fishing. His mother asked if she could make breakfast for me and I said sure. After breakfast she asked me if I thought she was attractive. I said, "Yes," and she asked if I would like to kiss her. Boy, did I. About five minutes later our clothes were off and she was on top of me on her bed.

It was wonderful but a little weird. I had masturbated by that point in my life but actual intercourse was truly a new and amazing experience. After I came my dick went so limp I was terrified that I would never have an erection again. Boy was I wrong. She and I had a relationship for about a year.

A *thirty-nine-year-old man* wrote:

My first time was really good, partly because the girl knew what she was doing.

We had been petting very heavily for several dates and I knew it would happen soon. One evening she was wearing a jumpsuit that unzipped all the way down the front. We went out on the back porch of her house and she unzipped her jumpsuit and stood there, waiting. I peeled the soft cotton flannel off her shoulders and just looked at her lovely body for several minutes.

Then we stretched out on the floor and after several minutes of foreplay she reached for my cock and guided it into her. She had been with several partners before and knew the way to make love. She showed me how to play slowly and we fucked each other for several minutes before I came.

A *fifty-eight-year-old woman* wrote:

The first time was when I was sixteen and my boyfriend was twenty. I was on vacation with my family and my best girlfriend, and he and my friend's boyfriend drove down to see us. He half forced, half pleaded with me to go all the way to prove I loved him, and that I hadn't been with anyone else while I was away.

It was in the backseat of his car, with my family's cottage just a few hundred yards away. Although he was very tender and kept telling me how much he loved me, it certainly wasn't as wonderful as I thought it would be. The car was cramped, and because I was a virgin, there was the usual first-time mess to clean up.

It did feel pretty great once the initial pain was over and I could feel his cock explode inside me. Although it would be a while before I experienced my own orgasm, it was really something to have this big strong man exploring my body, inside and out, and enjoying it so much.

A *forty-two-year-old man* wrote:

It was while I was in college when I was in my early twenties. I started to date a divorced woman who worked in a snack bar near campus. The first time we went out we went back to her apartment and started fooling around. I was surprised that she wanted it as much as I did. After that first time, we "did it" every time we dated.

One of the really fun things we did a lot was to shower together. Sometimes my dick would get hard from the excitement of just thinking about the next time we'd be under all that hot water.

A *forty-seven-year-old man* wrote:

My first sexual experience was a bit belated since I was probably nineteen or so. I was attending a local community college and had gotten a job as the lab assistant in the photo department. I'd asked a student to model nude for me and, amazingly enough, she agreed. After I took several photos of her I developed them and just stared, imagining—well, you know what I was imagining. A few days later she came to my house to pick up the pictures and to make me dinner. After dinner she took me to my bedroom and we did it. I still have copies of the photos.

And then there were these answers.

A *sixty-eight-year-old man wrote:*

The first time I had sex was in the back of my old car. I had taken a girl who worked in the same office out and she and I drove into the country and parked. I suggested we would be more comfortable in the backseat, and she didn't argue. I kissed her and soon we were "frenching" passionately. She made only nominal protests as I progressed into her panties.

After I had fingered her for a couple of minutes, she allowed me free rein. Since she knew I was a virgin, she opened my trousers and fished for my erection. She caressed it and soon I straddled her, in preparation to enter what was for me unknown territory.

As she aimed my cock at her wet, juicy opening I ashamedly poured all of my promised goodies all over her. I couldn't think what to say, so I said nothing. She gave a look of disbelief and asked if I had come and I just nodded.

She scolded me and said that she had really wanted me. I apologized for what had occurred and said that it was because it was my first time. I said to just wait and I would be ready again in a short while.

"How long will it take?" she asked and I said I would be rearmed and ready for action again in fifteen or twenty minutes. I have to give her credit, she didn't make a big thing out of the incident. After a few minutes, she recommenced stroking me, and in a short time, much less than the fifteen minutes I had expected, I was stiff. This time I made my first entry into the wet, willing, and waiting body.

Maybe it was good that I had had a premature explosion, since I was able to last quite a while, and we both built up into a climax simultaneously. After a suitable period of rest I managed to get it up for a third time and we did it once more. She congratulated me for being able to have three orgasms in a relatively short space of time.

A *seventy-seven-year-old man wrote*:

My first time I was in high school and going steady. We were both seventeen and virgins. We had done a lot of petting but had never gone farther than touchy-feely.

After our senior prom we headed for the local lovers' lane and our petting escalated to full intercourse. We were in my mother's 1936 Buick and somehow we left a stain on the passenger's side of the front seat. When my mother found it the next day I caught holy hell! On top of that, I hadn't been smart enough to use a condom and for several weeks I was scared she might have gotten pregnant. We were lucky that time, but I made sure to have condoms with me from then on.

A *forty-seven-year-old man wrote*:

My first time was at a drive-in movie. I was seventeen and had been dating this girl for about four months. We had been to the drive-in several times and had made out but never touched each other's private parts. One evening we went there on a double date and the couple in the front seat were going at it hot and heavy. Eventually the girl began going down on her boyfriend. My date and I were making out, too, but we were both looking up front from time to time, watching what was happening.

When the couple went to the snack stand, I unzipped my pants and asked her to suck me like the girl in the front had been doing to my friend, but she said no. I begged, and she began to stroke my cock. I came in a few minutes.

About a month after the first time at the drive-in the girl and I were back there with the same couple. My date was giving me a hand job then dipped her head into my lap, just as the couple in the front were doing the same. In a way it was sort of funny, looking back, because my buddy had been kidding me about not getting any oral sex while he was. On this night we were both getting blown, and I think we each started moaning louder than normal because we wanted to show off a bit. It was a short showing off for me, because I couldn't have lasted two minutes in her mouth before coming.

The next week we double-dated again with the same couple. While the girl in the front seat again began going down on her boyfriend I began exploring my date's pussy with my tongue and then finger. After a while I showed her a condom and she nodded. I slid it on, then thrust into her. Her blouse was open, but her bra was still on as I started fucking her. I remember looking toward the front seat and seeing two sets of eyes admiring our actions. They were kind enough to turn away when they realized that I had seen them. That time I was first! He had gotten blown first but I was the first to get laid. I treasured that condom and carried it around with me for months.

A fifty-nine-year-old man wrote:

We were double-dating and in the backseat of my friend's car. We were parked at an overlook doing some heavy petting when I got my fingers into my date. I just about burst my jeans but by the time I got them down, I had come in my shorts and no amount of anything would get my cock back up.

The couple in the front were sympathetic, as was my girl, but even though we dated for another year, I never got into her when I was hard. Looking back on it, that was probably a good thing, since we were not using any protection. The guy in the front seat on that famous double date wound up getting his girl pregnant.

A twenty-year-old bisexual woman wrote:

Which first time? The *first* first time, which was with a woman, or the first time with a man?

My first serious sexual experience was with my first girlfriend. We had been schoolmates, and after leaving school we gradually came out to each other through e-mail. After a while of meeting as friends and doing a bit of the London gay scene, we got together. Our "first time" happened, embarrassingly, in a pub toilet.

We were out with a group of old friends, none of whom knew about us, and were hence unable to kiss, hold hands, or be anything other than "just friends." So we nipped off to the ladies' loos and though we started off just kissing, we ended up having what amounted to sex, while hoping none of our mates was wondering what had happened to us. It turned out later that since we had taken so long, someone had actually joked, "Maybe they've eloped together!" That friend didn't know how right she was!

A year later I had several one-night fooling-about sessions with a guy friend that involved near penetration, but not real serious sex.

My *actual*, technical first time with a man happened a lot later, after a lot of varied sexual experiences, and so assumed much less importance in my mind. It was a bit of a nonevent really. It certainly didn't hurt, because, since I was a very active child, I don't think I had had any hymen for *ages* before that.

A fifty-year-old man wrote:

There are really two first times. Let me explain.

One first time was what you might call close-enough-to-intercourse. It was on New Year's Eve in 1970–71 during a snowstorm in the backseat of my father's big ol' Chrysler. The woman I eventually married and I had been dating for six months and the time was right. I was nineteen, she was eighteen, and it was the first time for either of us.

Up to that point in our relationship we had been getting hotter and hotter—grinding, feeling, etc., but that night it just wasn't enough. We just kept going, getting naked together and getting down to it. In actuality I didn't enter that night but there was lots of fingering and such. Technically and officially it wasn't the "first time" but I think we both agreed that after that night things between us were different. We had entered a new level.

The actual first time came sometime thereafter, again in the back of a car. It was quite anticlimactic—no pun intended. It was painful for her—bleeding, etc. and I came too fast—quite forgettable.

A sixty-four-year-old man wrote:

At the age of twenty-three, after approximately ten years of unsatisfied horniness, I was absolutely desperate and convinced that I would never get laid. Finally, one afternoon, I had a date with a girl whom I knew had had sex with a number of guys. My best friend Manny had been fucking her but they had broken up.

Linda and I had been obviously attracted to each other for a while and now that she and Manny had broken up, Manny had made it clear to me that he had no objection to my seeing her. He even let us use his place. We had a few drinks, started making out, and soon were both panting and sweating. Our clothing was gradually disappearing. I was down to my underpants and Linda was wearing only panties, but when I tried to remove them she stopped me and said, "I don't do that anymore."

Just my luck, I thought to myself, *she has to pick now to reform and decide to stop fucking around.* So, resigned to the fact that all I was going to be able to get was more heavy petting and a really bad case of blue balls, I continued sucking her nipples and stroking her cunt through and under her panties. We continued to get hotter and hotter, both sexually and physically (it was in the nineties that day), until I felt like I was about to explode.

Finally, frustrated beyond anything I had ever suffered before, I went to the other side of the room and knelt down on the floor facing the wall. I felt like a total failure. Here I was with a girl who had screwed around quite a bit, who was obviously as turned on as I was, and I *still* couldn't get laid. I don't think I had ever felt so bad about anything in my life. I was on the verge of tears and I certainly didn't want her to see me cry.

Linda came up behind me and, obviously concerned, asked me what was the matter. "I can't stand it," I said, trying to keep her from hearing the tremor in my voice. "I'm so hungry for you."

"But I was ready for you ten minutes ago," she said.

Confused by her earlier comment, totally at odds with her statement, and afraid to believe what she was telling me, I turned and looked at her. As I watched, she removed her panties and stretched out on the floor next to me, never looking away from my face. I mounted her and started to come even as I entered her. It was the fastest fuck I have ever had, but at that point in my life, absolutely nothing could possibly have been more satisfying.

WHAT WAS THE
BEST SEX YOU
EVER HAD?

M any of those who answered this question described a position, an activity, a game, or a toy as the "best." I can't help but wonder why that one time would stand out. Wouldn't they try the same thing again? To those of you reading and trying to decide how you would have answered this question, if you decide on one or more "best time," consider how you can make it happen more than once!

Other letters describe activities that might not be *your* idea of the best sex ever, but understand that these are the opinions of real people. You may read a letter and think, *No way! No real person ever did that!* I don't know, nor do I care whether each activity is accurately reported. Maybe some are fantasies of the best sex that might be. Even if they are merely fantasies, they are all tales of great sex for someone.

For me, describing the best sex I ever had is impossible. At different parts of my life, great sex had differing meanings. For example, in my still-virginal dating years, having a guy touch my breasts and get me all hot yet satisfied in some way was fabulous. Later, when I had fallen into a serious rut with my then-husband, doing something slightly out of the ordinary—which, sadly, happened rarely—was great. Now, since Ed and I share so much and can communicate so well, we make many of our experiences "the best." Okay, that's a cop-out, but it's the best I can do. Many of my respondents had the same problem.

A thirty-two-year-old woman wrote:

There's no specific "best," just many times with my husband. It is so *great* because there is total trust between us. We each know that if we are trying something new, and one of us isn't completely enjoying it, we can stop without guilt. The greatest thing about sex with my hubby, he is a *giver!* He wants me to climax every time and he feels like he isn't doing his "job" if I haven't! He is *not* at all selfish!

A forty-five-year-old man wrote:

What a difficult question to answer! I don't know that I could ever narrow it down to one particular episode—I know for sure I have lots and lots of fond memories. One of the things my wife and I have going for us is our honesty.

It all began one day long ago when I got us a day-use hotel room. I sent my wife there with the key, told her to read the instructions I had left her in the room and follow them to the letter. She did, including writing answers to a series of questions about what she thought I was going to do with her and to her and how she felt about it. I had made a list of possible activities including blindfolding, light bondage, fairly aggressive spanking, oral and vaginal intercourse.

Later I read the answers, learned a lot, and we've been communicating honestly and clearly since then. How fond a memory that day is—especially since she felt so close to me, too. She calls it one of our "special" times.

A thirty-eight-year-old woman wrote:

I feel that the best sex is when I feel totally excited and the person with whom I am making love is so into me and I am so into

him that it just flows. It feels so good with no inhibitions or holding back. Just pleasure.

A *fifty-four-year-old man* wrote:

The best sex probably was the time that I was stroking my wife's
clitoris and I kept doing it. She asked me to stop but I kept it up. I
also kissed her breast and sucked her nipple, but she told me to
stop so she could focus. She began to wriggle and move wildly
after several minutes while I slowly continued to rub her. All of a
sudden she started shaking violently. I continued to stroke as she
came once and then a second time. I mounted her and as my
penis slid into her vagina, she came again. When I started to climax, she shook and went crazy and cried. It was fantastic. We do
it that way occasionally now, but it isn't the same as that first
time.

A *fifty-four-year-old man* wrote:

That has to be my first lover. She went wild when she climaxed,
digging her nails in my back and biting my shoulder. She not only
gave me pleasure but made me feel like a great lover.

A *forty-five-year-old man* wrote:

I guess that would be when my partner and I climaxed at the
same time while I was inside her. This is difficult to achieve for
us, because she usually cannot orgasm through penetration
alone.

We started by mutually masturbating each other while kissing,
then we went at each other orally in the sixty-nine position. As I
got close to coming, I changed positions and continued cunnilingus
to bring her closer to orgasm. We finally got into the missionary
position and as I slowly fucked her, I continued clitoral stimulation, first with my finger and then with an Eroscillator. When I felt
her muscles contract around my cock I knew she would soon
come, so I began thrusting a little faster to bring myself close to
climax. I could tell by her moaning that she was going to come,

and when she did, I released my warm juice into her and we embraced each other as we simultaneously reached orgasm.

A twenty-five-year-old woman wrote:

That would have to be the first time I was with my current partner. It was great because it was the first time I actually climaxed while having intercourse, not just from masturbation.

We were sitting on his futon, me straddling him, and he was deep inside me. I began slowly at first to rock my hips, causing an amazing sensation. His pelvic bone rubbed my clit at just the right spot. I began going faster as the sensation grew. He had his hands on my hips, lifting me, then pulling me down on him with every thrust. I could feel him getting harder inside me and then for the first time I felt that familiar sensation rushing through me but this time a man had helped with it. A moment later he reached his.

A twenty-five-year-old woman wrote:

I guess the best was the first time I actually had an orgasm during sex. I was with my boyfriend and I told him that I was not able to come from just fucking. One night he told me to rub my clit and he ate me out until I just about died. I felt my muscles begin to contract and release so he put his penis in me and began thrusting. He flipped me over and I began to ride him hard and fast. I completely soaked him. There was a huge wet spot on the bed on either side of him where my come had slid down his sides.

A twenty-seven-year-old woman wrote:

The best sex was after a day of running errands. My boyfriend and I had spent all our time in the car teasing and rubbing, grabbing kisses whenever we could, and giving quickie hand jobs. After hours of doing this we reached home and left a trail of clothes all the way to the bedroom. It started off with him behind me, and ended up with me on top. I felt him get hard about two minutes after he came the first time so we went at it again. The sex and feeling that amazing emotional connection between us made it the best. Oh, and when we finally went back downstairs, the gallon of ice cream we had bought had melted all over the kitchen counter.

A *thirty-one-year-old woman* wrote:

It was a one-night stand, full of oral sex, which I like best. I had six orgasms that night and, believe it or not, that was the first time I had had even one with a partner. I have never again had that many in one night.

A *thirty-one-year-old woman* wrote:

It was with my first lover, a guy I started going out with in high school. He had bright red hair with a flyboy haircut, fair skin, and light freckles. A friend and I were at a high school football game when he and his friend came over and started flirting with us. He was a smooth talker and we started dating.

The sex started with kissing. My God, he had beautiful lips. They were full and puffy and he was very experienced. I had no intention of losing my virginity at the age of sixteen but he made me want it *so* bad.

After the several make-out sessions during which we kissed until I was crazy, I finally let him slowly move on to other locations. He started to use his hands, caressing my shoulders and following with his lips. He nibbled lightly on my ears and slowly licked a moist path along the tendons of my neck. My heart pounded and I could hear myself breathe and moan. Eventually we got to doing it, but the earlier make-out sessions, the ones before it all got complicated, were the best.

A *thirty-three-year-old woman* wrote:

I was with my lover in his car and it just happened. We had been together all evening and I felt really horny so I started to give him a blow job. He couldn't concentrate so he pulled off the side of the road. We moved to the backseat where he fucked me passionately and hard, just the way I like it.

I don't know why it was as good as it was. Perhaps it was because it was the first time we had done it in a car, or the first time we had pure raw sex.

A *thirty-five-year-old woman wrote:*

We had started with oral sex with him fingering me at the same time. I could feel pleasure building until we finally moved to slow passionate lovemaking. I needed more, however, so I took control, got on top, and started moving up and down. I quickly discovered that that didn't do it so I started a slow rocking and rubbing back and forth. Oh yeah, that was the ticket. I increased the movement, and I came so hard that he had a small puddle on his belly. That was my first female ejaculation.

A *forty-one-year-old woman wrote:*

My husband and I rented a motel room with a big tub surrounded by mirrors. We had dinner then went to a strip club for drinks, so we were pretty horny by the time we got back to our room. My husband used wine and ice cubes on my vulva in the hot tub and all the while we watched ourselves in the ceiling mirror. We made love two or three times.

A *forty-three-year-old woman wrote:*

My husband had some medical problems and he was paralyzed for eight months. After he was able to make love to me again and we were able to get into the swing of things, he fulfilled one of my fantasies.

One night, after his shower, he stood before me with a swollen cock and told me to suck him. I got down on my hands and knees and sucked his big cock into my mouth until he was almost ready to come. Suddenly he pulled back, ordered me onto the bed, and told me what a bad girl I had been. He told me I needed to be fucked up the ass good and hard. He knows that I love it when he's dominant and strong.

As we both knew I would, I protested but that got me a good hard spanking until my ass glowed for my "insolence." The spanking turned me on so much that my pussy was dripping and he rubbed some of my juices on my asshole and started to push his huge cock into my ass. He told me to rub my pussy as he fucked my ass and continued to tell me what a bad girl I had been, spanking my ass occasionally until I came. By the time I was done coming, I was slamming my ass hard onto his cock. He pulled out and came all over my back.

My ass was sore from the fucking, my ass cheeks were red and hot, my pussy was wet and slimy, and I was totally satisfied.

A forty-seven-year-old woman wrote:

That must have been the time with my ex when we were in the closet in my room with my son doing homework in the next room.

A fifty-eight-year-old woman wrote:

Every time I have what I think is the "best sex" I'll ever have, something comes along to top it! One of my favorites was an encounter on a flight from Boston to Denver. I was sitting beside a very handsome young (thirty-six to my then-fifty-one) man in first class and we talked and enjoyed each other's company. We shared a lovely dinner, drank too much champagne and wine, flirted, and just got to know each other for the entire four-hour flight.

Although we were both in relationships there was a definite connection that seemed too good to waste. When we landed, we decided to get a nightcap, and of course one thing led to another. We ended up back at my apartment, making love all night long, in every way possible. We were so exhausted when morning came that we each called our office with an excuse for being even later than we already were. Then we spent another few hours continuing our explorations of each other's body and found new ways to bring each other pleasure.

The fact that there were no expectations, just spur-of-the-moment pleasure, and that we could be totally uninhibited with each other must have made it the incredible night it was, one I'll always treasure.

A *thirty-one-year-old man wrote:*

My favorite sex was with a girl I'd been casually dating and fooling around with for about three months. Lots of petting, etc, but no hard-core nooky.

She and I arranged over the phone that she would come over and watch a movie on the following Friday. I told her, "Just so you'll know, I'm planning on getting you drunk and seducing you."

"Oh, really?" she replied with a giggle. "I might just let you."

Well, she came over dressed to the nines in a favorite white silk top of hers, a knee-length, schoolgirl dress with stockings and garters. She was a stunning nineteen-year-old woman, too, with auburn hair down to the middle of her back, full breasts, with a tiny waist and full-figured hips. She had a perfect hourglass figure, which this night she'd enhanced with a bustier. When I commented on how amazing she looked, she purred, "Well, you said you were going to seduce me."

She had designed herself to be my fantasy, and she was. We used lots of positions, and she looked perfect to me from all of them. My only regret was that she left in the middle of the night and it was one of our last encounters before she started dating a friend of mine. I will never forget that evening and hey, who's complaining.

A *forty-two-year-old man wrote:*

The best was probably with a gal I dated before I got married, who just loved sex in all of its forms. She loved to be on top, and to have digital anal penetration while we were going at it. She almost always ejaculated, and we'd take one or two towels to bed to catch her juices. She had heavy breasts and loved to sit on my dick and swing her boobies around then have me suck on them as we made it.

A forty-two-year-old man wrote:

I remember a dinner party twelve years ago when I did it with my best friend's wife in a bathroom. We had been having an ongoing flirtation but we both knew that it shouldn't happen. That night it finally did because we could wait no longer.

We slipped into the upstairs bathroom, very rushed, but very horny. There was an urgency about it, a fear of getting caught but a wild instinct driving us on. After a quick release, and in the hurry to return to the table, she couldn't get her panties back on so she slipped them into my pocket. I kept them and only threw them out last year!!

Anyway, later that evening I felt sure we looked guilty and satisfied as we sat opposite each other at the table, both grateful that the lights were low. As the other six guests (my wife and her husband included!) were noisily debating something or other, the lady slipped her stockinged foot up the inside of my thigh and got me hard again in seconds. She was so cool, not even making eye contact with me! We've screwed again only twice in the twelve years since that happened.

A fifty-year-old man wrote:

I've only had sex with my wife. We met in high school, dated through college, and have been exclusive through twenty-six years of marriage. There are several great sexual episodes we've shared over the years, so it's tough to pick out just one.

When the mood is right we can really go nuts. I can think of one such evening when I borrowed my friend's video camera and set it up in our bedroom. We put on a show and just "did" each other. Great foreplay, sixty-nine, and fantastic mutual orgasms. I think we both kind of liked the idea that we were on camera and, although the video was fun to watch, it didn't do justice to our activities.

Other memorable episodes were usually preceded by watching a porno movie. When we were younger, and our kids were small and in bed by 8 P.M., I'd rent assorted X-rated films for us to watch. My wife always fought the whole concept since it was definitely against her Catholic school upbringing, but inevitably we would have great, outrageous, no-holds-barred sex. Unfortunately, because of the kids, we haven't rented a porn movie in several years. Thank goodness for HBO with shows like *Real Sex* and *Sex and the City.*

A fifty-two-year-old man wrote:

For almost a year my wife and I had a relationship with another younger couple. Our first time together the naked brunette straddled my leg and brushed me with kisses. I felt a strange sensation on my thigh, like being gently tapped with a finger. When I looked to see what it was, I saw that her vagina was totally dilated and she was dripping juices like a leaky faucet. She quickly impaled herself on my erection and all four of us began fucking like wild animals. That was one hot memorable moment in our sex life.

A seventy-seven-year-old man wrote:

This is rather difficult for me to answer since, for me, sex is always "good." However, with my present partner, our first time was the best because it was so unexpected.

I had driven her to an out-of-state wedding and on our way home we stopped overnight in a motel. We got the last room available and it had a single, king-size bed. It was a bit daunting since, to that day, we hadn't been sexual with each other.

When it came time to go to bed, instead of going into the bathroom to get ready, she suddenly said, "The hell with it, let's do it!" and stripped naked. By the time I got out of my boxers, I had a full-blown erection. We engaged in foreplay for twenty or thirty minutes before we "consummated" the act. By the time I finally ejaculated she had orgasmed at least twice.

Afterward, over cigarettes, she said to me that somewhere

during the drive she had decided that the new bride wasn't going to be the only one who had fun that night.

A *twenty-five-year-old woman wrote:*

It was New Year's Eve 1999 and, since it was our first New Year's Eve together, my fiancé and I got a hotel room. For the first time ever I had bought some sexy lingerie but I was a little embarrassed because I weigh 289 pounds. Well, I put it on while he was in the bathroom. When he walked in and saw me his jaw dropped. I loved the way he looked at me.

Part of what made it so special is I was three months pregnant so I couldn't drink. My fiancé really likes to drink but he didn't because I couldn't.

One more thing. I had also gotten a disposable Polaroid and we took "naughty" pictures of each other. He made me feel so special that night and when we finally started to make love he was gentle and sweet.

A *fifty-one-year-old man wrote:*

That has to be the first time that my wife Kathy and I had sex. It was about twenty-eight years ago, before our marriage, while we were students in college. We were in a class together and, although I had noticed her earlier, I had thought that she was already taken since she always sat next to the same guy in the lecture hall. I had just been rejected by a long-term girlfriend and was pretty lonely.

I got in a big argument with the professor one day in class, because he wanted to change the requirements midsemester. The whole class was mad, but since it was a required class and everyone else was afraid of angering the guy, no one else spoke up. I guess I argued pretty well because the professor backed down and went back to the original requirements.

Kathy came up to me later that day in a private place on campus and, after she congratulated me, we talked for a long time. She was different from my ex, who was Hispanic and dark skinned, a flamboyant actress type. Kathy was quiet, Irish, very white skin, brown hair.

We ended up at my dorm room later that night and, since my roommates were gone for the weekend, Kathy asked me if I wanted her to stay the night. Well, one thing led to another. I cannot remember exactly how we ended up in my bed naked but we did. She told me how much she liked my body, clean cut, with short hair, as compared to other longhaired males of the 1970s. She said that she had been watching me in class, despite her other male friend. She also giggled and said that she liked the shape of my ass.

She started kissing me all over and then went down on me. Later I remember making love to her with me on top with her legs wrapped around me. I looked down at her and saw the Irish freckles on her face and breasts. I felt great joy and we've been together since.

A *fifty-five-year-old man wrote*:

The greatest night of sex was with my wife when, after eighteen years of marriage, she finally decided to let me perform oral sex on her. We must have made slow, sensual love for close to three hours. Her comment upon tiring was, "Why did I wait so long?"

A *fifty-six-year-old man wrote*:

I remember the day well. It was after about ten years of marriage and our eight-year-old daughter was away. For the first and only time my wife and I made love three times in one day.

The first was right after we woke up and the second was when I came home from work at lunch. She undressed me and stroked my penis and balls. Since she still had her clothes on, I just pulled her panties aside and entered her. The third time was when I got home that evening. While we watched the news on TV she rode me, and had two orgasms, one after the other. For both of us each orgasm was better than the last.

A sixty-two-year-old man wrote:

There are two equal candidates.

The first was in the 1970s. I had an affair with a married lady, a tiny little redhead who was a sex machine. We had a "dirty weekend" once where we screwed or had some kind of sex about ten times in two days. Upside down, backward, oral, anal—she had a soft wet pussy that was big for her size and she could go for a long time before coming. She gave head like no other and swallowed it all, which made *her* come. I have never experienced quite the same feeling again, having a woman moaning and coming and sucking me dry all at the same time. I still get aroused thinking about it.

The second "best sex ever" was with my current partner of twenty-five-plus years who loves to be screwed from behind and, of course, I love to do it. When her beautiful bum is up, her head down, and we are connected, she moans, screams, cries, and pushes against me until she explodes (as do I). And it keeps getting better.

A sixty-nine-year-old man wrote:

The best was with a girl whom I dated for three or four months before discovering she was a high-priced call girl. Subsequently our relationship continued as, by then, I was able to accept the situation. As a matter of fact, I found it stimulating to hear of her liaisons each day. We lost contact when I was appointed to a job in Europe.

A forty-six-year-old man wrote a long answer:

This was several years ago. My wife Veronica and I had signed up for an erotic weekend at a friend's bed-and-breakfast. We didn't quite know what to expect, but we were game for just about anything.

We arrived at about two-thirty on Friday afternoon. We weren't yet settled in when it was time for our three o'clock appointment with Claudia, the sensuous massage therapist. I knew that this wasn't going to be an ordinary therapeutic massage and I was more than ready. Since Veronica was still unpacking, I volunteered to go first.

Claudia had one of the small hotel rooms set up with a massage table and a CD player with soft, relaxing music. She had me lie facedown on the table and warmed some oil between her hands. She began with my toes, then moved up my legs to my butt. As she was rubbing her way up my legs, she reached between them to touch my penis and balls. Boy, it felt great! After about thirty minutes of massage and teasing she had me turn over.

I rolled over onto my back and Claudia placed a small towel over my eyes to put me into a total relaxation mode. As she had on my back, she started at my toes and moved up my legs. As she rubbed up my thighs, she would lightly touch my now partially erect penis. She spent about fifteen minutes on my upper body. While on my chest, she would pinch and tease my nipples. Now I know why this was advertised as a sensuous massage!

I was so hot and my erection was obvious. Claudia purred softly, then applied a healthy amount of oil and began to directly massage my penis. My eyes were still covered and that added to the sensual nature of everything.

After about two minutes, I came in her hands! It was wonderful but the best part was she didn't stop! I was almost floating off the table and she was still going at it! After what seemed to be forever, she lightly caressed my penis and chest, cleaned up the mess I made, gave me a kiss on the cheek then left for a few moments' break.

I had been lying there for a while when my wife walked in. Although she hadn't seen my orgasm she must have known what had happened. With a little tease in her voice, she commented that I certainly seemed to have enjoyed the massage! I got up and told her that Claudia would be back in a moment. She asked whether she'd enjoy it and I told her, "You'll have the best massage ever!"

I left the two women alone for about half an hour, then returned to the massage room. It was obvious from the way Veronica was writhing on the table that Claudia had given her the same treatment she had given me. I joined in massaging my wife's beautiful body until Claudia whispered into my ear, "It's your turn now." She told me that the table was strong enough to hold both of us, then slipped out of the room.

Not wanting to wait another minute, I pushed my wife's knees up to her chest and climbed onto the table. We were two horny greased lovers at that moment. Since I had already come once, I was ready to go on for a long time, and so was she.

Suspecting what the massage would do to Veronica, I had brought one of our favorite toys, a thick vibrator, and I had it all lubed up and ready to go. I inserted it into her vagina and she almost bounced off the table. I kissed and suckled one of her breasts while gently moving the vibrator around. After about five minutes, she began to come and it was just a wonderful sight. It was a great evening and the great start of a wonderful retreat!

A fifty-one-year-old woman wrote:

The best sex I ever had was with a man I had been seeing for a long time. It started early in the day when he called me at work and told me he was thinking about me kneeling before him and sucking his dick. I agreed that it was a wonderful idea, and, for the rest of the day, I was completely turned on and couldn't wait to get to him.

When I got to his house that evening we sat and talked for a little while and then he invited me to join him in the shower. We "helped" each other get good and clean. It was so erotic to touch his smooth, soapy body . . . I thoroughly enjoyed it. When I finished, I got out, dried off, and waited for him kneeling on the bedroom floor. He's very sweet and romantic so when he came out he offered me his hand with the intention of taking me to bed.

I pulled him to me and ran my hands over his body, letting

him know that I intended to fulfill the promise that I'd made earlier on the phone. He got very hard inside my mouth and I was so turned on by that. He pulled me up and guided me onto the bed where he asked me to get on my hands and knees. One of my favorite positions is "doggy-style" and he's wonderful.

Two things made that evening so great. First is the fact that I love this man with all my heart and second is the way he works so hard to please me. I know he wants me to enjoy our lovemaking and that makes me feel loved in a way I've never felt before. He's an excellent lover. I feel very lucky.

A *sixty-eight-year-old man* wrote:

I've thought about this question and I've settled on a recent experience with a lover who came to visit. We started necking standing in my kitchen, and she felt me get hard against her tummy as I slid my hands down and cupped her ass, pulling her against me. We went upstairs and stripped each other. She sort of half sat and half lay back on the edge of the bed as I stood between her legs and alternated between sucking her nipples and kissing her mouth. As I would lean over to kiss her, the head of my erect cock would graze her cunt lips.

Eventually I knelt, pulled her ass to the edge of the bed, and licked her clit and slit, teasing her wet opening. I set my cock head at her entrance and talked to her as she worked on "sucking" it into her pussy. I'm pretty large so I went slowly, allowing her to adjust to my cock. Opened and lubricated, she finally drew me in all the way so my balls were against her butt.

We spent a long time with me fucking her as hard and deep as I could, and with her riding my cock and leaning over to have me suck her nipples as she came several times. Eventually I asked to fuck her from behind. She knelt and arched her back, presenting her now sopping cunt to me. I slid in and she begged for me to give it to her hard and deep, then yelled for me to come. I did with huge, heartfelt spasms.

Immediately after I came she slid off my cock, sucked the

come off my cock head, and lay back, asking me to fuck her with a dildo I had given her. I did that, too, and licked her clit as I did. As she started coming again she reached down and grabbed the dildo, fucking herself with hard deep strokes as I licked her. She came and came.

A twenty-one-year-old woman wrote:

I love to take control, so the best sex I've had so far was when I initiated it, undressed him, then myself, then performed oral sex on him while he stood there with his hands in my hair, his legs shaking. After he came in my mouth, I kept him hard and had him sit on the couch where I straddled him and slid down onto his erection, moving as hard and as fast as I could. He let me have total control and he enjoyed it as much as I did. We learned a lot that night and much of it has carried over into our sex life since.

A thirty-two-year-old man wrote:

There are really two times that come to mind.

The first was on our first anniversary when my wife and I made love in front of a fireplace in a small inn in Vermont. I used the head of my penis to stroke her clitoris, and we both came together, one of the few times that ever happened.

The other was when I gave her a Yoni massage from a book I had read on Tantric sex. I kept her stimulated for over an hour and never even touched her clitoris. Finally she came, screamed (also a first), and actually ejaculated. I came with no stimulation to me, just from having seen her. Unbelievable!

A fifty-four-year-old man wrote:

The best was when my wife and I made love in the basement on a deck-chair mattress. We used a flavored lotion that got warm with body contact. I rubbed it on my cock and on her tits and I have never come so hard in my life.

A thirty-six-year-old woman wrote:

I'm not sure exactly how to answer. Perhaps my best was casual sex, I'm embarrassed to say, with a guy I met at a bar while in college. We went to my dorm room and had sex for two or three hours. I was so turned on because he just kept saying how gorgeous I was and how beautiful and good tasting my pussy was. All that talk just got me going.

A twenty-six-year-old woman wrote:

The best sex I ever had was on the basement floor. I was flat on my back and he was kneeling between my legs. He was able to be inside me and still use his hands to roam all sorts of fun places.

A nineteen-year-old woman wrote:

My best time was the first time my husband and I had sex. We had gone out of town and were staying in a hotel. It was the first time I had had any sex since I was raped as a young teenager.

My then-boyfriend knew about my past so he went very slowly and was really understanding. He didn't rush me or force me into anything, just kissed me very slowly from head to toe. He massaged me and touched every part of my body. It may have not been very good by someone else's standards, but to me it was the best just because he was so considerate of what I had been through.

Afterward we held each other and talked and then eventually did it all again. We stayed up all night just making love and cuddling and enjoying being together. He replaced all those bad memories with thoughts of a night of wonderful loving.

A forty-eight-year-old man wrote:

A long time ago there was a secretary at work. Even though we were both partnered we'd been flirting for months. After the Christmas party that year I gave her a ride home and we ended up parking. We did all kinds of stuff, from oral to several creative positions with each of us reaching several orgasms. It was wicked, bad, and wrong—and yet so right. We met three more times and she gave me excellent oral each time. We also shared great anal sex.

On what we agreed would be the final time she asked that we do it in her boss's office. I will never forget the sight of her perfect ass bent over her boss's desk. She was wearing garters with lace-top black stockings, and the sight of lifting her skirt and revealing all that was incredible.

A *twenty-two-year-old man wrote:*

My best, although there are lots, was a night of real lovemaking, licking, rubbing, and kissing each other all over, watching each other's reactions, engrossed in giving one another pleasure. It had started with just a kiss, but once we kissed, we couldn't stop. It was slow and sensual. I think it was so great because it was all about making each other feel good, and showing one another how much we loved giving each other pleasure.

A *sixty-year-old man wrote:*

I once had a very turbulent secret sexual relation with a colleague from the office, a twenty-six-year-old dark-skinned girl from Malaysia. She was really attractive and sexy with soft skin and coarse, dark pubic hair.

One day we fucked for several hours outdoors in the long grass in a fruit orchard. I took her that day in every possible way. She gave me blow jobs and I made her come with my mouth and fucked her with my tongue. What was best was that at the end of the day she decided she wanted to blow me, have me come in her mouth, and swallow. I kissed her madly and we both shared my come. This is the most intense sexual experience I ever had.

A *thirty-eight-year-old man wrote:*

My girlfriend and I went to a nightclub for drinks and a dance one evening. She had on a tight top with a full-length zipper and a tiny little swishy skirt. I asked her to zip the top up only half way so, since she didn't wear a bra, I could see her tits jiggle. Wow, did they. When she danced I could clearly see her big, hard nipples. Since she wasn't wearing panties, I was able to play with her cunt on the dance floor by pulling up the front of her skirt. On the way home she undid her top all the way and played with her tits while I watched.

Later, while I tried to drive, she pulled up her skirt and masturbated to orgasm. Well, I had to stop at the side of the road at the airport so she could give me a nice head job.

A fifty-nine-year-old man wrote:

Probably the first time my wife sucked me off would qualify. She put a little too much suction on and I think she sucked out some of my brain cells.

A thirty-three-year-old woman wrote:

Actually, the best sex that I've ever had is a toss-up between masturbating and a lover I had about five years ago. He was seven years younger than I was and he really knew what to do and how to do it. It was great because it was the first time I was given oral sex and he knew just how to do it. He licked and sucked until I was dripping wet, then made me come like I'd never come before.

A fifty-one-year-old woman wrote:

I lost a bet with my husband one day several years ago. I don't even remember what we bet on, but had I won he'd agreed to do the housework for me while I sat and did whatever I pleased. If I lost I had agreed that he could do whatever he wished to me for one night. Well, I lost, and he chose to give me an enema, then have anal sex with me.

I'd always refused his requests for anal sex because it was embarrassing and I thought it would be icky. He was intuitive enough to have figured out that I really wanted to try, but was afraid of making a mess. The enemas he gave me while he played with my clit and put a vibrator in my vagina made me incredibly hot so that, when he lubed his cock and slowly entered my ass, it felt exciting, with little pain. We play like that often now.

A *forty-seven-year-old woman* wrote:

My lover and I did it on my former boss's office desk while the cleaning lady was in the outside office. I had on a two-piece suit with stay-up stockings and high heels but we were so hot for each other we couldn't wait. He opened my blouse, unhooked the front clip of my bra, then pushed up my skirt, unzipped his pants, and rammed into me. My lover was pumping me really hard and my tits were bouncing when we both exploded.

Afterward we had to attend a retirement party for one of our colleagues and my boss was there. All through dinner my lover and I couldn't stop looking at each other, the smell of sex still on our bodies. He told me later that all he could think of during the meal was me, lying across that desk with my tits bouncing and my legs wrapped around his neck. That was just one of the many "best sex" scenes we have shared.

A *twenty-six-year-old woman* wrote:

Although I have had great sex with my boyfriend of eighteen months, I'd have to say the best sex was with someone I'd been wanting for a long time.

In my senior year of college—before I even knew what an orgasm was—I'd been having an ongoing flirtation with a guy. He was adorable—dimples, perfect smile, broad shoulders, great body, funny—and he made no move to hide the fact that he was attracted to me also. Finally, about a week before I graduated, we had sex—crazy, I've-been-wanting-you-forever sex. No orgasm for me—like I said, I didn't know how to yet—but damn, it was good.

I have spoken with him a few times since, but I never did anything else with him. I think that's part of the attraction: a long-awaited consummated flirtation, never to be repeated. Makes it kind of sacred.

A *thirty-six-year-old woman* wrote:

The best sex I ever had was a couple of years after we were married. One night out of the blue, as we finished the dinner dishes and in what seemed like slow motion, my husband came up behind me, gently pressed his front onto my back and pushed me up against the kitchen counter. One arm slid around my waist while the other reached out with my hand to turn the light off. Our fingers entwined and he wrapped them around my waist, too.

He softly and gently kissed my neck and shoulders until my knees got weak and my skin was warm and tingly. Then he slowly turned me around and moved his kisses to my mouth. He lifted me onto the counter, unbuttoned my sweater, and un-hooked my bra (do guys go to school to learn how to do that one-handed in a second?). Sweet warm kisses landed on my nipples with that little bite he does to make my back arch.

He scooped me up and settled me on the gliding rocker in the nearby family room. Sliding my pants and panties off in one swift motion, he started to kiss and suck my toes, quickly working his way up my legs until he was between my thighs. I was aching for him to touch my clit and when he did I came right away. He entered me and, after a few kisses, I came again. The gliding motion from the chair was nice for him too. Eventually we wore out that chair but we just could not find another spot like it.

A *twenty-three-year-old woman* wrote:

One night when I got off work at about one in the morning I walked in to find my house lit just with candles. My favorite cocktail was sitting on the table next to a pretty nightie and a note that said, "Put this on." I collapsed on the couch totally tired and not really in the mood for loving. I was sad to be disappointing him, but then his hands slid over my shoulders with the cool sensation of gardenia-scented lotion. I love gardenias.

He didn't say anything but continued to massage me until I was about to doze. Eventually I found myself on the floor on my favorite mink blanket. I hadn't even noticed how wet I had become but he sure did and worshiped me with his tongue until I couldn't take any more. We spent the rest of the night reaching one peak after the next and woke up cuddled together on the floor, wonderfully exhausted.

WHAT WAS THE WORST SEX YOU EVER HAD?

The best answer I got was from a fifty-six-year-old woman. She wrote:

I cannot conceive of it ever being bad.

Bravo for her! Most of us, however, have had unfortunate experiences. Many of those who answered mentioned a time when one or the other wasn't in the mood. Making love when it's just not right at that moment is a drag.

Quickies also rank up there. What's a quickie? Sex that doesn't last long enough to satisfy one partner or the other. Leaving someone "hanging" is really poor.

For me, I have two, both during the one-night-stand period between my divorce and my relationship with Ed.

The first was with the professor of a weekend course I took. We ended up in a hotel room and it was really quick. I don't remember the sex part but what I do remember is that he never took off his undershirt or his socks. Why the socks remained I don't know, but he told me that he loved to embarrass his cleaning lady with the semen stains on his T-shirt. Needless to say, he told me this after-

ward. Had I known what a jerk he was I wouldn't have . . . Actually
I probably would have, since in those days, I was keeping count of
how many men wanted to go to bed with me. After my divorce,
with my self-esteem at a low point, it seemed important that men
find me attractive enough for sex.

During that period I spent an evening with another man who told
me in pretty graphic terms that he was "well hung." I guess he
thought I'd get a thrill out of his oversize equipment. Unfortunately
he thought his size made up for a lack of foreplay. I was still dry, and
his oversize penis never really fit. Suffice it to say, I ended up at my
gynecologist's office, abraded and very sore. Since this was before
AIDS and I was on the pill we had not used a condom, so the doctor gave me a shot of penicillin for good measure.

I have to relate one other story. I was in college and my then-
boyfriend and his best friend were both members of the ROTC.
They went off for six weeks of summer training and both my soon-to-
be hubby and his friend were super horny when they returned. The
friend and his girl, having no place to make love, ended up in the
woods, doing it on the grass. They found out afterward that they had
been lying in a patch of poison ivy. We all laughed about it later—
much later. They said they didn't know which was worse, the terrible
itchy rash or trying to explain to their parents how they got it.

Here are some of the "worst times" sent in by the respondents to
my survey.

A twenty-three-year-old woman wrote:

I had a really lame one-nighter with a guy three years younger
than I was. We fumbled and messed it all up—it was a total joke.
He came in about five seconds and I wasn't excited at all. To this
day I don't know why I was even there in the first place. I was
really confused about who I was but that's no real excuse. I think
even today he would still suck!!!

A twenty-seven-year-old woman wrote:

I should have known that he was just an incredibly selfish lover because he was a bad kisser. He climbed on before I was even remotely close to ready, and didn't really care whether I was turned on at all. He barked out orders assuming I wanted only to please him. First and last time with him.

A thirty-two-year-old woman wrote:

The first guy I ever had intercourse with was the *worst*. I was eighteen and the guy was twenty-six. He was very selfish! At the time I had no idea how bad a lover he was . . . now I do and I feel sorry for him! I never climaxed when I was with him. He was a Slam, Bam, Thank You Ma'am kind of guy. As long as he got off he couldn't care less how I felt. There was no real foreplay, nothing to make it fun for me! The saddest thing about the entire experience was that I thought it was normal. I thought all the things I'd read and heard were fairy tales. Fortunately I've learned otherwise since.

A thirty-four-year-old woman wrote:

I'm almost six feet tall, overweight, with large breasts and a sizable ass but I don't mind it at all. It's who I am and that's that.

I had a one-night stand several years ago with a guy I had talked to frequently but only dated once. After we made love—no, *fucked* would be a better term—he said that he had never been with a big woman before and was just experimenting. He made it clear that sex was very different with a larger woman and his tone said clearly that he didn't like it. To hell with him!

Fortunately for me, lots of men disagree—most don't care what size I am, just how good a lover I am, and that's fine with me.

A thirty-eight-year-old woman wrote:

I remember the one time a guy tried anal sex. It was painful, even with lubricant. I was totally unsatisfied, and felt violated and used.

A forty-one-year-old woman wrote:

The worst is when I accommodate my husband but can't get myself in the mood.

If you're not in the mood, don't do it. If you do have intercourse, you will end up resenting it and him, gritting your teeth and letting him do what you feel he has to do. Hogwash! That makes the entire experience so negative that afterward you vow sex won't happen again for a while. And it doesn't. Been there, done that!

Maybe it's time you suggested that a bit more foreplay or a bit less frequency might make it better for both of you. Try to think of things that might make it all more fun—a bit of alcohol to relax you both, then some teasing, dirty talking, toys, games, fantasies. All can turn the tide. If you lighten up and play a bit, each time becomes easier and more fun. Here's a letter that illustrates the man's point of view.

A forty-one-year-old man wrote:

Bad sex is whenever the woman is just doing it just for me and going through the motions. I'd rather just jerk off. If she's not enjoying it the way I am it turns me off.

A forty-two-year-old woman wrote:

One time I had intercourse with a guy who was very rough. I told him to slow down but he didn't seem to hear me or maybe he just didn't care. Needless to say that was the first and last time we ever slept together. Oh, and can you believe that when I said no, he wanted to know why? So I told him. I hope his next lady benefited.

A forty-three-year-old woman wrote:

I was offered a ride home by a person whom I thought was a friend. He pulled over on the side of the road and ordered me to suck his cock or I could get out and walk. I had never performed oral sex so I walked home. It was several miles but I'll tell you, it didn't feel bad at all.

A fifty-one-year-old woman wrote:

A few years ago I was separated from a guy I had had a very serious relationship with. In attempting to get over my feelings for him, I began seeing someone else. I liked the other man and we'd been friends for a while. Eventually we decided to have sex. I wasn't in love with him and since being in love with a guy is important to me, the sex was not particularly enjoyable. What made it worse was that he worked so hard to make it good for me. I pretended to enjoy myself but I'm sure he knew. We ruined a good friendship.

A *twenty-five-year-old woman* wrote:

In an effort to have a romantic evening, my boyfriend and I did it in the park. It would have been nice but we were on an incline and we kept rolling to one side. There were stones and sticks under my back, and it was too cold. It seemed like it would be so romantic but everything about it was just wrong. Actually, we've laughed about it since so maybe it wasn't so bad after all.

A *thirty-year-old man* wrote:

I once had sex with a new girl after a great meal and movie. She projected the image of being the perfect sex partner and I thought things were going to be fabulous. The problem was that I didn't come. The "perfect sex partner" couldn't make me come.

A *thirty-one-year-old man* wrote:

The worst sex for me is really a tie.

Once I was with a woman who barely moved and sent that message that says, "I'm letting you do this." That was lame. I had sex with her a second time to test the waters. Nothing was different, so I ran.

The other time was really worse. I was drunk at a party with an equally drunk young actress. After lots of fooling around, teasing and playing, I fucked her. My judgment was impaired, and she was too drunk to be put in that situation. We had unsafe sex and I felt incredibly guilty about contributing to her burgeoning reputation as a slut.

A *thirty-two-year-old man wrote*:

The first time I had intercourse was the worst by far. It was bad because I really didn't care anything for the girl I was with, so it was pretty empty feeling. The only redeeming thing about it was the fact that we did it in front of two other couples, and I found that very exciting. With the main event lasting about two minutes, I'm sure it was the worst sexual experience for the girl as well.

A *thirty-six-year-old man wrote*:

Unhappily the worst sex I have is with my wife. She doesn't want to try anything, doesn't like oral or even touching my genitals.

A *forty-eight-year-old man wrote*:

Sadly, my current lover is probably the worst. She will not talk about sex in any form, not our sex life or sex in general. We have straight missionary sex, and not very much fooling around before or afterward. She has nice boobies, which I love to play with, but she doesn't like me to touch her. All in all, sex with her is pretty off-putting, due to her attitude about it. Other than the sex, she is a lot of fun, and we have good times together, but the sex sure does detract from our relationship, at least from my perspective.

There may be more going on in these relationships than we know: a power struggle, outside-the-bedroom issues, and so forth. There are, however, ways of *tempting* a woman to become more experimental. Making love in the shower, playing with chocolate sauce or maple syrup, reading sexy stories—all can help, but it takes work and cooperation. It's really sad that these two men can't establish better relationships.

A *thirty-nine-year-old man wrote*:

I met this girl when I was about fifteen and she was twenty-three. She teased me and used me for her pleasure and wouldn't return the gratification. I had the worst case of blue balls ever.

A forty-year-old man wrote:

The worst was at a massage parlor. I had gone there for a real massage and found it to be a hand-job place. Yuck.

A forty-five-year-old man wrote:

My first time was the worst. I was so excited that I came as soon as I entered her.

A sixty-nine-year-old man wrote:

The worst was my very first love affair in my late teens, when I was unable to control my ejaculation and was scorned by the girl. She told all my friends about it, too.

A seventy-seven-year-old man wrote:

The worst sex I ever had was with my first wife. I had just gotten out of the army at the end of World War II and we were living with her parents. Her father, who thought that all sex was fornication (her mother must have raped him in order to conceive), made it difficult for us to have intercourse in the house. My wife could get quite vocal during the act.

We had found a spot in a cemetery where we could go when we wanted to have intercourse. One night, when we were both "in heat," we headed for the cemetery but as luck would have it, it started to rain. We ended up doing it in the car, a 1935 Chevy coupe. Between fighting the gear-shift lever and the close quarters, it was a disaster.

A seventy-eight-year-old man wrote:

The worst was when our kids were teenagers and were prone to barge in or knock. This kept my wife and me on edge, and we seldom orgasmed that way.

Hint: Get a hook-and-eye lock for the bedroom door and use it every night, whether you intend to make love or not. And tell your kids that you want, and need, private time so unless the world is ending, leave you alone.

A *thirty-year-old woman wrote:*

After my ex-husband and I separated, we still had sex. It wasn't good at all because I realized that I no longer had feelings for him. It was just awful.

A *fifty-one-year-old man wrote:*

The worst I can remember was my first time. I was a skinny, gawky virgin who had been a nobody in high school so I joined the marine corps on my eighteenth birthday. Although my body was transformed in marine corps recruit training, a year later I was still a virgin.

I went to a party with some marine corps buddies and there was a whore there. We were both drunk and I accidentally admitted to her that I was still a virgin. She thought it was very funny and said that I was not going to leave the party a virgin. She fucked me there for free. It was terrible. I came fast and she laughed.

A *sixty-two-year-old man wrote:*

I had sex with a hooker in Hong Kong many, many years ago. What made it so bad? She had no interest, could not even fake it.

WHAT IS THE MOST EMBARRASSING THING THAT EVER HAPPENED TO YOU WHILE MAKING LOVE?

I have to relate a story told to me by a friend many years ago. When she was four or five she had a glow-in-the-dark picture of the Virgin Mary beside her bed. One evening she decided that her parents needed a visitation so she turned on her bedside light and held the picture over it until it glowed brightly, then she tiptoed into her parents' room. I'm sure you've already guessed what they were doing. That was probably *their* most embarrassing moment.

For my writers, there were a few common threads. Farts, both rectal and vaginal, ranked at the top of the list.

Close seconds were premature ejaculation and impotence.

A *seventy-seven-year-old man* wrote:

My most embarrassing sexual experience happened on my honeymoon with my first wife. On our honeymoon night, I was so anxious that I ejaculated as soon as I had penetrated her. Talk about premature ejaculation! I was so embarrassed! We did make up for it later that night but I'll never forget that disastrous first time for us.

A *thirty-one-year-old man* wrote:

I had problems with premature ejaculation in my early twenties. That always made me feel pretty limp, literally and figuratively.

If you have such problems, try using a condom to dull the sensations and slow blood flow. If you already use one, add a second. It really helps.

A *thirty-two-year-old man wrote:*

My wife had been home alone one weekend while I worked on an emergency project at work. She had spent the whole day reading erotica, watching dirty home movies, and getting very aroused while waiting for me to get home to take care of her needs. I, on the other hand, was furious that I had to work that day. When I got home I was angry and in no mood for sex, but my wife looked so sexy lying there in her lingerie, practically making a puddle on the sheet.

The embarrassing part? Well, I tried but was not able to rise to the occasion. Although my wife was very understanding, I felt really awful, like a failure somehow.

A third common thread was being interrupted by . . . well, let them tell it.

A *twenty-seven-year-old woman wrote:*

We had a roommate who didn't believe in knocking, and he walked in on us when I was on top. I ducked under the covers so fast!

A *thirty-one-year-old woman wrote:*

Actually I think the most embarrassing was one night right before my second husband and I were married. He was on top, just ramming away, when he must have heard my bedroom door jiggle, so he grabbed the covers and rolled off the side of the bed so quickly that I didn't really know what was happening. When I looked around, I found myself lying there naked without hope of a cover, facing my eight-year-old daughter! The rat was quietly scooting deeper under the bed! Later he had the nerve to laugh!

A sixty-nine-year-old man wrote:

My lady and I were interrupted by the conductor while making love in a compartment of a European train.

A forty-two-year-old man wrote:

The most embarrassing time was when my son, age two at the time, came in and sat on my back while I was atop my wife. When I collapsed, mortified, he yelled, "More horsie, Daddy."

A fifty-year-old man wrote:

I've got to go back to when I was in college.

It was a nice summer day and my girlfriend (now my wife) and I were tooling around on my little red motorcycle enjoying the sunshine, hormones flowing through our young bodies. We parked the bike by a beach, walked a bit, and came upon a beautiful grassy lawn overlooking the water.

Well, one thing led to the next and before you knew it we were on the grass, butt naked, getting it on. The only thing missing was violin music and rose petals. Out of nowhere a voice screamed, "Get out of my backyard!"

We looked up and saw this old woman running toward us, yelling and screaming, "Where do you think you are?" and "What are you, a couple of dogs in heat?" etc. We jumped up, grabbed our clothes, and started running, with about a twenty-five-yard lead on the old lady. We stopped long enough to put our pants and her top back on and ran back to the bike, underwear in hand, people staring at us, and this old woman still charging after us screaming!

We jumped on, kicked the starter, and took off, never looking back! What a memory. We laugh about it to this day, although it wasn't so funny at the time.

A nineteen-year-old woman wrote:

The most embarrassing thing that has ever happened to me

while having sex was when my husband, then my boyfriend, and I got caught by the cops. We were at a place that some of our friends had gone to and so we thought it would be okay.

We had just barely gotten started when the cops pulled up. They knocked on the window and so I hurried and pulled my pants back on. Let me tell you, it's not an easy task in a car anyway, much less when you're nervous as hell. My husband acted very casual about the whole thing, like it was no big deal, while they searched my husband and the car and my purse, looking for drugs I guess. We didn't get into any trouble, but it was so embarrassing.

A forty-seven-year-old woman wrote:

My partner and I were on the floor in my office when the cleaning lady started to open the door. Quick as a flash my lover scrambled behind the door and I quickly started typing on my computer. The lady walked into the room and said, "Oh, I didn't think anybody was here."

"I was working late," I said, and asked whether she could come back later. Shaking her head sadly at the idea that someone had to work so late, the cleaning lady agreed and left. The whole time, my lover was standing behind the door with his pants down, grinning at me.

A forty-seven-year-old woman wrote:

The most dreadful was one year when I was home for vacation from college. My father came into my room while I was in the shower and found my then-boyfriend sound asleep and naked in my bed. Oddly enough, we hadn't even done anything that day. He had just dozed off because he was exhausted.

A thirty-six-year-old man wrote:

We got caught in the middle of the night by the police doing the deed on a jungle gym in a local park.

Here are a few more unique experiences.

A *twenty-seven-year-old woman* wrote:

I remember when my ex's penis hit my gag reflex while I was performing oral sex and I threw up. Ugh!

A *twenty-eight-year-old woman* wrote:

The worst was when his dog lay next to us on the floor chewing the crotch out of my panties. I guess it wasn't too bad, though, since my boyfriend and I didn't stop.

A *thirty-two-year-old woman* wrote:

I fell asleep! I'm laughing just thinking about it. It was a few days after I first met my hubby, and we had been up all night and all day for two days straight. Nothing but partying, clubbing, and fucking! We were in the middle of going at it again when I just fell asleep. We were kissing and I accidentally bit down on his tongue when I dropped off. I felt terrible, but he was good about it and understood!

A *forty-seven-year-old woman* wrote:

My new husband and I were on a long bus trip to a family re-union. It was well after dark and both of us were really bored. Although it was midsummer the air conditioner was revved up and it was really chilly so we had been cuddling beneath a thick blanket. My hubby unbuttoned my sweater but kept it closed, then slipped his fingers up through the leg hole of my shorts. He made me come a few times but I was pretty quiet about it. I re-member that I covered it up with a make-believe coughing fit so violent that one of the ladies on the bus asked if I wanted some water. I politely declined.

Then I went to work on him. He had on sweatpants so I grabbed his already hard cock. I hadn't realized that he had picked up his coffee cup and when he came he made an odd sound and dropped the cup in the aisle. As several people bent over to help him clean up the mess, I quickly closed my eyes, removed my hand, and acted like I was asleep. Later, as I wiped my messy hand on the blanket, I realized that it wasn't our blanket. Ouch.

A twenty-two-year-old man wrote:

Once, before I'd lost my virginity, I was getting it on with a girlfriend. Trying to be casual, I unzipped my pants and, since I wasn't wearing underwear, my cock got caught in my zipper. She realized what had happened and tried to help.

I didn't want to stop what we were doing so I continued to eat her pussy while she tried to get my penis free. Actually she made me come just by trying to remove my cock from my zipper. The final result was that the only pair of trousers I had were covered in a mixture of blood and come.

A thirty-three-year-old woman wrote:

I had had an IUD installed and a few night later I was really in the mood so I initiated things and got my boyfriend really hot. I told him that I wanted him to take me then and there and as he did the weirdest look came over his face and he got up from the bed.

It turned out that the IUD string had "stabbed" his member. I was really embarrassed and it kind of put a damper on our night.

A fifty-one-year-old woman wrote:

I had a wicked headache one night so my hubby went to get a cold compress and put it over my eyes. As I lay back to let the cold do its work he started to kiss me softly and cuddle me. He was being so sweet and attentive that I wanted to do something for him, too. We moved to the sixty-nine position and the closer I got to having an orgasm, the more my head pounded. He was near, too, and I didn't want to stop.

I didn't make it. I vomited all over him, before he had a chance to come.

A sixty-two-year-old man wrote:

While home from college, my girlfriend and I were hard at it in my bedroom when the bed broke—the slats fell out. We were fixing it when my folks came home and it was no secret what had happened. My mother fled, the old man said "fix it," and things were quiet around the dinner table for a few days.

WHAT'S THE MOST WONDERFUL THING THAT EVER HAPPENED WHILE MAKING LOVE?

Several people answered this question by saying that they discovered that they were actually in love. Take care. Love and lust are often confused. I will admit that in the first blush of lovemaking, particularly when I was quite young, I made that mistake and continued to see a boy who was really wrong for me. Fortunately I didn't make any permanent commitments, but I'm afraid that this confusion contributes to our enormously high divorce rate.

Sex is great, and Mother Nature sees to it that we know it. Hormones provide animals with some strong drives, and we humans are no different from other life-forms.

With that said, the emotional connection with a partner during and after lovemaking is unsurpassed. Tears of joy, cuddling, warmth, and caring all combine to make lovemaking a most fabulous activity.

A fifty-one-year-old woman wrote:

Turning to look at him in the aftermath and seeing tears in his eyes is just terrific. He told me how lucky I was to come as hard as I do and how proud he was to be able to give me that much pleasure.

A twenty-seven-year-old man wrote:

The most wonderful thing is the explosive intermingling of love, desire, and lust that can incinerate you and your partner.

A fifty-one-year-old woman wrote:

Approximately three months after I started seeing my current partner, we had made love and he was holding me after we had both come. For the first time in my life I felt that I was in love and loved. It was a wonderful feeling and one that I won't ever forget.

A thirty-one-year-old man wrote:

Hearing someone I'm in love with say my name is my favorite and most wonderful moment.

A fifty-nine-year-old man wrote:

Feeling close to another human being is great. It's kind of like becoming one. It took months of close communication to set the stage but that first time and every time since have been worth anything in the world.

A thirty-two-year-old woman wrote:

I realized that I was in love while making love to the man who would become my husband! The realization that this was more than just sex made the experience just a little more wonderful!

A fifty-year-old man wrote:

Aside from conceiving our three children, I'd say just the closeness with each other, and the total complete sense of oneness is the best. We still appreciate and enjoy that aspect of our relationship.

A sixty-two-year-old man wrote:

The most wonderful thing that ever happened to me was when, still joined together after a warm, romantic lovemaking session in a small London hotel, my wife agreed to marry me.

A twenty-six-year-old woman wrote:

The most wonderful thing is the eye contact that my partner and I have during sex.

Then there are the orgasms themselves.

A twenty-one-year-old woman wrote:

The best is the feeling of having an orgasm with an erect penis inside me.

A nineteen-year-old woman wrote:

The most wonderful thing that happens to me during sex is when my husband and I climax at the same time. It's very rare, but when it happens, it's great.

A twenty-eight-year-old woman wrote simply:

MULTIPLE ORGASM. [The capitals were hers.]

A thirty-eight-year-old woman wrote:

To have one orgasm after another is so intense.

A thirty-five-year-old woman wrote:

I would say that female ejaculation is probably the best that has happened. It drives my hubby nuts.

A fifty-four-year-old man wrote:

Mutual climax is right up there.

Making children was the most wonderful thing for several women. For example:

A thirty-six-year-old woman wrote:

The most wonderful thing that has happened while making love was the creation of my two wonderful boys!!!

A forty-seven-year-old woman wrote:

Making our son.

A twenty-five-year-old woman wrote:

Her name is Faith Angelica and she will be two years old in June.

What did others who responded to the survey have to say about the wonders of great sex?

A sixty-eight-year-old man wrote:

Making videos of the lovemaking and then watching them with my lover is just wonderful. We love both activities.

A thirty-two-year-old man wrote:

There are times when I am able to slow down to the point of being on the verge of orgasm, but I haven't yet fallen off the plateau. I am frozen except for a gentle pulse from my penis that courses through my body every so often. I simply lose all sense of time and space and I'm only aware of my pleasure and my wife. It doesn't get any better than that.

A thirty-three-year-old woman wrote:

The most wonderful thing that ever happened to me was when I saw the look of love in my boyfriend's eyes as I was taking him in my mouth. He had never come in someone's mouth before and he thought lovemaking was now complete for him.

A forty-five-year-old man wrote:

My most wonderful was the first time I had a partner go down and give me fellatio.

A fifty-eight-year-old woman wrote:

It's all been pretty wonderful, but one of the best was getting to live out a fantasy we had talked about—making love on the beach on the Riviera.

It was our first trip to Europe and we had talked about the scenes from *To Catch a Thief*: the location, the characters, etc. When we went to Cassis in the south of France we sort of relived the movie, but with more detail.

I gave my lover a blow job on the rocks by the shore with the village in the distance and lights flickering in the harbor. The understanding French locals kept their distance but enjoyed the view, I think.

A thirty-nine-year-old man wrote:

The best was when my wife became willing to role-play during sex.

A forty-seven-year-old man wrote:

Learning how to pleasure my partner and being able to explore her lovely body (every nook and cranny) was the most wonderful.

A fifty-two-year-old man wrote:

One night my wife, a male friend, and I made love and orgasmed about seven times. Terrific!

A seventy-seven-year-old man wrote:

The most wonderful thing that happens to me is hearing my partner say "Don't stop, I'm coming!" and having her throw her arms around me while she orgasms. That is the greatest thing I can think of.

A twenty-one-year-old woman wrote:

I'm still waiting to experience my first orgasm but I think the feeling of holding a man tight while he climaxes is so wonderful.

A sixty-nine-year-old bisexual man wrote:

I discovered my submissive second self.

MASTURBATION

The Ways, the Games, the First Time

DO YOU
MASTURBATE?

Okay, let's move on to masturbation. Haven't you ever wondered whether real people do? Well, they do!

Let me give you some statistics based on the surveys I received. This is probably a more liberated group than the average but, with that in mind, here's what the numbers said.

Of the respondents, 98% of the men said they masturbate, while 96% of the women stated that they do. Of those who do masturbate, 24% of the men and 25% of the women said they masturbate at least once a day, while 58% of the men and 55% of the women said they masturbate at least once a week.

As you might expect, 62% of the women said they use toys, while only 45% of the men claimed the same.

Just over 80% of both the men and women thought their partner knew that they masturbate but, strangely, only 60% of the men and 68% of the women thought their partners did it.

A *twenty-six-year-old woman wrote:*

I do it nearly every day and, although I was brought up to believe it was wrong, I love it. I didn't touch myself for a long time until I suddenly discovered all kinds of amazing things about myself. Now I know what I like and what I don't like and now that I know I can tell my boyfriend, too.

I'm damn good at it, too; like anything else it gets better with practice. I've done it so much that I've become multiple orgasmic. I've even tried to see how many climaxes I could have; I had six in about half an hour before passing out cold.

I try to make it different and interesting every time. Sometimes it's just a quickie to help me sleep; sometimes, I drink a little wine, read a book—*Vox* was my most recent—and "romance" myself. I just recently bought the iRabbit, a vibrator extraordinaire, and it's terrific. I prefer my hand, though—human contact is always better than a tool. I enjoy masturbating in front of men, too, if they like it.

A *thirty-four-year-old woman* wrote:

Yes, I do, and the frequency depends on the time of the month. The week before my period, I masturbate probably two or three times a day. The week after my period, I may only do so once or twice all week. During my period, I have learned that masturbating relieves my cramps so the second and third days I may masturbate seven or eight times! It's purely therapeutic, of course (evil grin).

I have a vibrator to make it easy especially if I am in a hurry. I always close my eyes and fantasize completely unrealistic scenarios (like having a threesome with my husband and another male, or being the guinea pig in a scientific sex study). If I am not in a hurry, I like the easy stimulation of a soft spray of the shower on my clitoris. Nothing like a little good clean fun!

A *sixty-eight-year-old man* wrote:

I masturbate whenever I feel the urge, about three to four times a week. I use lubricant, getting very hard and pulsing, edging toward ejaculation for a long time. Stimulation? It varies, sometimes it's on the phone or with a cyber partner, sometimes alone.

I even have videos of myself masturbating, which excites me. I love the sight of my cock, hard and ready, and I love watching it come as I feel the spasms.

A *twenty-one-year-old woman* wrote:

I masturbate almost every day. More than anything else pornographic movies get me in the mood, and erotic stories often work well, too. My imagination also plays a big part in it. Music doesn't usually play into my masturbation, but I know that it does with my partner.

A *forty-seven-year-old man* wrote:

I masturbate three times a week, sometimes more, generally lying down in bed fantasizing. Sometimes I like doing it to your short stories, Joan, and I also enjoy good porno movies. My hand works just fine, but occasionally I add my wife's vibrator. Sometimes I lube with baby oil, sometimes with hand cream. I guess it just depends on my mood.

My wife knows, but not "overtly." She does know that a few times when she did not want to have sex and I was desperate, I jerked off in bed with her next to me, sometimes talking dirty to me, sometimes helping a little with her hand.

She doesn't admit that she masturbates, but sometimes I have noticed that, when I return from a business trip, her vibrator has been moved. I know it's bad to peek but I do. I wish she'd share this with me because I think we could add it to our love life.

A *thirty-two-year-old man* wrote:

I masturbate every other day or so using lubricant. I like to read porn on the Web and sometimes I use a butt plug for added stimulation.

A *thirty-six-year-old woman* wrote:

I masturbate occasionally. My husband didn't used to mind but lately my sex drive has taken a dive so if I were to masturbate without him involved, he'd likely be annoyed.

A *nineteen-year-old woman wrote:*

I masturbate three or four times a week. I usually just have to rub my clit to get off, but occasionally I insert a finger or two. I just do it whenever the urge hits me as long as the baby is asleep.

My husband says he doesn't masturbate but he does buy porno magazines and I suspect that he jerks off from time to time. I don't really mind. Show me a man who says he can go three weeks without any and I'll show you a liar. Hey, as long as he can stay satisfied without needing another woman I don't care how he does it.

A *twenty-six-year-old woman wrote:*

I have masturbated since I was twelve. Now I do it once a week or so. I start out by watching a sexy movie or reading a steamy book until I am completely aroused. Then I use clitoral stimulation only until I have an orgasm. It usually only takes a few seconds to get there because I know exactly where to touch. I have never used a toy but I admit I am curious about vibrators. Someday I may have the courage to actually buy one.

A *twenty-two-year-old man wrote:*

Of course I masturbate. Even when you're in a relationship, I think you still have to do your own thing once in a while. I believe that you have to love yourself and be open to self-experimentation to be able to love and be experimental with someone else.

Once when I was at university I wandered into some nearby woodland and placed all my clothes into a bag. I placed the bag in a ditch, and walked about five hundred yards from it so there was no way I could get back to my clothes in time if someone saw me. I just lay down in the mud and masturbated. I was there for ages. I just kept getting close to coming and then stopping and starting again. I wanted to increase the danger, I guess. I ended up coming all over myself after about fifteen minutes.

A sixty-year-old man wrote:

I like to look at myself naked in a mirror, or gaze at a picture in a magazine, a TV film, a woman or girl outside, or at my partner lying in bed next to me. I fantasize a lot about having sex with different women, in different poses or situations while doing myself, and I often take as long as I can before coming.

When I come while looking at my female neighbor sitting and relaxing before the large window on a chair in her living room, I just feel great, maybe because I think about the possibility she can see me doing it. Sometimes I even do it in sight of a woman passing by. It gives a tremendous tension just wondering, *Has she seen what I did?*

Sometimes I try to get an erection without using my hands by sticking my penis into a small detergent drawer of the washing machine we have. When I stand upright it's exactly level with my penis and it is the same width. I put my penis in and close the drawer as far as I can so my penis is held by the machine. Then I start moving forward and back and . . . I get a huge erection. After that my hand takes over.

I think it is good to do it as often as you can and enjoy it, since then your sexuality is kept alive and you feel in a better shape. My wife often masturbates next to me in bed and that turns me on a lot! It's great to masturbate while watching a woman doing it at the same time.

A fifty-nine-year-old man wrote:

I don't masturbate alone much because I do not have to, except when my wife is sick or something. I do, however, masturbate as part of sex with her. What feels particularly good is the last few seconds before coming. The routine goes like this.

She lies on her back, spread wide enough so I can straddle her left leg at the thigh. I put the fingers of my left hand inside her and my right hand strokes my penis until it comes on her tummy or tits. Then I collapse on top of her and rub my come between us. We spend a few moments, then clean up.

We use toys sometimes, too: vibrators and dildos usually. Sometimes I put the little one inside her and my penis tight next to the vibrator. She is not very adventurous but goes along to please me. She likes me inside her.

My wife doesn't masturbate alone either. Her first husband just used her as a place to put his come and then rolled over and went to sleep. She did not have her first orgasm until after we were together and she damn near blew a gasket the first time she came. She can help bring herself to orgasm at times, but generally she likes me to do it for her.

A *twenty-year-old woman* wrote:

Masturbation for me varies from a couple of times per week to twice a day, depending on my mood and location. At the moment my boyfriend is quite tired a lot of the time and goes to bed earlier than I do, so sometimes I need a little more satisfaction than I'm getting. Also, I find it very hard to climax during sex or any way other than with my own fingers.

I tend to masturbate in the morning, or late at night. I usually read on-line erotica or find some porn. I put a cozy rug over my desk chair, sit down half cross-legged, and remove my slacks. I find something to insert inside myself—a tube of mascara with a tightly closed lid works wonders. I used to masturbate only with my right hand, with a very specific stroke. The needs of on-line porn (I have a right-handed mouse) have taught me to use my left also, with a slightly different movement.

I find some images or stories that fit my mood, and alternate between using the mouse with my right hand and stroking my clit with my left and using my right hand to move the object inside me. It usually takes me around twenty minutes to come, but it can take much longer if I'm tired.

A *fifty-one-year-old woman wrote:*

The moments leading up to the orgasm, that excitement in all my nerve endings followed by that feeling that nothing could stop the rush, is the best thing ever.

I am particularly turned on by my nipples. I touch and rub them until they become turgid, then pinch them between my fingers, and pull on them until I'm really hot. Then I move one hand to touch my clit, pressing down on either side so that the little head pops up. I lazily circle as I dip inside my cunt for juices, then things accelerate and I come. It feels like an immense release of all my powers, as if I'm giving them over for a touch of paradise.

A *forty-seven-year-old woman wrote:*

When I masturbate, I like to pretend that my lover sneaks into my room and starts kissing me from the toes upward under the sheets. Eventually I dream that he performs oral sex on me. It makes me come every time.

A *twenty-two-year-old woman wrote:*

I masturbate occasionally, when I read, watch, or think of something that makes me horny and I don't have someone to take care of that need.

Orgasms are usually dependent on clitoral stimulation for me. I have two vibrators. I insert the one into my vagina and put the smaller one on my clitoris, a pretty quick and simple way to climax.

A *twenty-five-year-old woman wrote:*

I begin by rubbing my clit until I start to open up, then I slide my fingers in and stroke my g-spot faster and harder until I orgasm.

I have done it in front of my boyfriend and often rub my clit while we are having sex. He seems to like watching and will even buy magazines to get me aroused if I am not feeling sexual.

A *twenty-seven-year-old woman wrote:*

My masturbation routine is usually to read something sexy, any-thing from straight erotica like yours, Joan, to all kinds of fetish magazines. I imagine myself in the story and focus on my clit, rubbing as I read until I build to an orgasm.

A *twenty-eight-year-old woman wrote:*

I do it in the shower with a handheld shower massager but I would rather have a partner join in instead of doing it alone.

A *thirty-year-old woman wrote:*

I find that when I pleasure myself it's too fast and over too soon so I don't do it often. I read about people enjoying the pleasure for a long time but for me it's over within five minutes.

My husband encourages it and I know he would love for me to put on a show for him. Unfortunately I just don't feel comfort-able performing a show that is only going to last five minutes.

A *thirty-eight-year-old woman wrote:*

I masturbate almost daily. I enjoy the calm feeling after the re-lease, which for me is very fast. I usually use the middle finger of my right hand or a vibrator to rub my clit.

I own a bag full of expensive toys, most of which are good concepts but don't really work—butterflies, ben wa balls, vibrators with fancy tops. I prefer my simple vibrator with the speed on slow.

I also love my big dildo. It's rubber, two inches wide, and eight inches long with a suction cup at the bottom. What I love is the feeling of it first entering me, and I love to stand it on its suction-cup base on the side of my bathtub.

I am not able to orgasm through intercourse only, because it never lasts long enough. Consequently masturbation is part of our routine every time. I enjoy masturbating while his cock is pressed up against my vagina, or while I'm sitting on top of him, rubbing myself to orgasm. As soon as I feel release from clitoral stimulation, I almost immediately come from intercourse, and I'm able to "ride the waves" as I climax over and over again, for as long as he can remain hard inside me.

My husband says he never masturbates on his own but he has played with himself once or twice with me. I find it so erotic to watch a man pleasure himself. It gives me insight as to what he likes and what works for him.

A *fifty-four-year-old woman wrote:*

To get in the mood for my daily masturbation session I think of one of the men I've talked with on the Net whom I have special feelings for. I'll stretch out on the bed, sometimes with a rubber dildo or sometimes just using my hand stroking my clit, and relax and fantasize about how it might be with him there with me.

Sometimes I masturbate in the morning when I first awaken. I'll lie there half asleep, using one hand on my satin sleep shirt to caress my nipples while the other steals down to my mound, allowing my fingers to slip into my wetness. I slowly stroke my clit dreaming of my chosen partner, imagining him beside me there in bed.

I've asked some of the men I speak to on-line about if it would turn them on to see me masturbate for them, because I thought it might be a turnoff thinking they weren't enough for me. Surprisingly to me they were very positive about it.

A *fifty-eight-year-old woman wrote:*

I masturbate several times a week when I'm alone, but less often when my partner and I are together, although we do like to do it together. Sometimes we even do it over the phone since ours is a long-distance relationship.

A *twenty-five-year-old man wrote:*

Sure, I masturbate from time to time. When I was married my wife knew and at first she thought it was insulting and gross. It took a while but I convinced her it was a good thing to do. Eventually she grew to like it and wanted to watch. Now that we are divorced I have heard from her several times as a friend that she appreciates my teaching her to be less inhibited.

A *twenty-seven-year-old man wrote:*

My routine is to think of a girl I know. A lot of times it is an undergrad I am tutoring or someone I see around the campus. I imagine being seduced as I try to tutor her. At other times I dream that I'm seducing a pretty little freshman.

A lot of times, though, I am tricked into a compromising situation and raped by a woman with a strap-on. I use a lot of lotion and, as I stroke, my other hand cups my testicles, my back arches off the bed, and I scream very very loudly!

A *thirty-year-old man wrote:*

I have masturbated at least three times per day since I was twelve, and about twice a week before that, starting at age nine. Just to see what it would be like, I masturbated fifteen times in one twenty-four-hour period when I was fifteen.

I typically rub my cock while in the car on the way home, or discreetly under the desk at work. Sometimes women in SUVs or other tall vehicles will observe me while my car is stopped at a light.

When I get home I enjoy reading erotica or looking at pornographic images as my cock hardens and my balls cinch up. I will then often rub my asshole and penetrate it with a finger, the top of a shampoo bottle, or a rounded wrench handle.

A *thirty-two-year-old bisexual man wrote:*

I like to lie back, lube myself up really good, and slowly stroke myself with a tight grip. I usually read erotic stories and get close to climax, then slow down, and continue doing this until I can come at the same time as the characters in the stories. Sometimes I use an anal vibrator when I masturbate, and that provides incredible sensations that lead to explosive orgasms.

My wife knows I masturbate, and she often asks me if I have masturbated that day. If I have, she asks me to describe what I did. She occasionally asks me to put on a show for her. That's really exciting.

She, too, masturbates and it turns me on in an instant when she tells me about it. I especially like it when she tells me she got so hot thinking about me that she had to go into the ladies' room at work and rub her clit. When she tells me this, I usually attack her before she finishes.

A forty-year-old man wrote:

I seldom masturbate. Occasionally my wife asks me to do it while she watches. At those times I like to sprinkle powder on my inner thigh and my willy, then I gently rub it back and forth against my thigh until I'm there. A lot of times I don't finish because she hijacks my bone for her own fulfillment!

A forty-two-year-old man wrote:

Even if I have sex with my squeeze, I still masturbate at least once a week.

My lady and I like to play with each other nude. Playing with her breasts while she plays with my nipples is the surest way for me to get erect. Frequently she doesn't care whether she gets penetrated (or at least so she says) so we go into the bathroom and she plays with me while I masturbate. I love for her to suck and nibble on my nipples while I bring myself off.

My imagination will suffice most of the time to get me erect, but I really enjoy reading stories, like your books and stories on-line.

Stories with sexual violence always get me erect, as do stories involving threesomes and female double penetration, and wife swapping.

A forty-two-year-old man wrote:

I masturbate about once a week and I usually watch my ejaculation in the mirror. I frequently coat my left palm (I'm right-handed

so doing it with my left feels better) with cold after-sun cream, or
something similar. I come when I squeeze buttocks and thrust
cock up and forward while slowly rubbing around tip and rim until I shoot toward mirror.

My wife enjoys masturbation as well. Often when I am at work
Saturday mornings she rings me at the office to tell me she's doing it or that she's just come. Boy do I hurry home!

A forty-four-year-old man wrote:

I do it only two or three times a week because I like to wait until
I haven't come in a while. I enjoy the feeling of a full erection,
where my cock is really hard and throbs a bit as I stroke it.

A forty-five-year-old man wrote:

The best is when I use both hands to simulate oral stimulation.
Sometimes I shave all of my pubic hair off and masturbate when
I'm finished.

A forty-seven-year-old man wrote:

Often I wake up early in the morning and my hand just seems to
wander downward on its own accord. Then I begin fondling and
pleasuring myself. I really do enjoy reading erotica and/or watching video clips from the Web. The more turned on I get, the
more intense my orgasm(s) will be.

I sometimes use a Hitachi Magic Wand with a come-cup at-
tachment that slips over the head of my penis and gives me a
very intense, incredible orgasm.

A forty-eight-year-old man wrote:

I can control my level of excitement precisely. Sometimes I will
keep myself at a high state of arousal for a long time by masturbating almost to the point of ejaculation and then letting it rest
while I do something else. Then, when I come back to it (which I
always do), I'm ready to explode. I also love the feel of my penis
leaking pre-come in my skivvies, which it'll do for hours after I
masturbate and don't come.

A fifty-two-year-old man wrote:

I masturbate almost daily, usually when I get home from work. I open a cold drink and sit down in front of the computer to browse some Internet porn. I usually start out "dry" (sans lube) and as the excitement builds, I add a lube called ForPlay that always makes things feel extra sensuous. I like to start with a very light touch and gradually get more tactile, working just under the glans, teasing the hell out of my cock, holding things right on the edge. When I've found a couple of pictures that really excite me, I download those, revisit them, and take things to their natural conclusion.

A seventy-seven-year-old man wrote:

I masturbate mainly because it allows me to last longer when my wife and I have intercourse. If I've already come I can give her much more satisfaction.

A seventy-eight-year-old man wrote:

I masturbate two to three times a month. It feels better if I am viewing images or videos and I often use a vibrator, which can cause a very intense orgasm in thirty seconds. Sometimes my mind is enough, coupled with a wife who is extremely sexy and beautiful, even at seventy-five.

My wife not only knows I masturbate, but she prefers to do it for me herself if she can't have sex for some reason. She is a love.

A twenty-six-year-old woman wrote:

A great big turn-on for me was watching my boyfriend mastur-bate. It was several months ago and I talked him into doing it the way he does when he is alone.

He undressed, sat naked on his sofa, and began pulling on the head of his penis. I watched as his penis began to respond to the manipulation, and before long he had a nice erection. The head of his penis was really swollen as he held the shaft and be-gan stroking very slowly. He then rubbed his scrotum and testi-cles with the other hand as the stroking got faster and faster.

I got real close so I could see the action and watch the clear pre-come fluid seeping out as he stroked. His legs shook and he moaned as he pulled hard but slowly on the penis shaft. Finally he pulled down on the shaft and held it there as the semen shot out in short but powerful spurts. It was amazing to watch.

A twenty-one-year-old woman wrote:

I don't masturbate, per se, when I am alone. I prefer phone sex because my boyfriend is a long distance away. We start off with him teasing me saying he refuses to get naked. From that point, I'm the one who has to get things moving and it usually ends with both of us having a wonderful climax.

A thirty-year-old woman wrote:

I often fantasize about my partner fucking a girlfriend of mine. With that picture in my mind I rub my clit with my right pointer finger until I climax.

My partner does not like it when I do it. He says he thinks I am cheating.

A thirty-nine-year-old woman wrote:

I masturbate too many times to count. Frequently I shave my pussy and then tie my ankles and one wrist to my bed with crystal nipple clamps, an anal plug, and a vibrating dildo in place.

I fantasize that I have been kidnapped for some bad boy's pleasure. He teases me with his tongue and I use my free hand to caress my body pretending that it is him. I suck and lick my nipples (yes, I'm really big and I can do that) pretending that he is forcing me to be a bad girl. Frequently I come several times before I'm exhausted.

A sixty-nine-year-old bisexual man wrote:

What turns me on is a very mixed bag. Sometimes I visualize my wife in various sexy outfits and sky-high heels and at other times I am cross-dressed and am being fondled by a man.

This last letter isn't exactly on topic, but it's a wonderful picture of a great sex life.

A *thirty-six-year-old woman* wrote:

My husband and I masturbate together and by ourselves when we need or want to. Personally I like all areas busy: anal, vaginal, clit, and nipple manipulation.

I like to keep things interesting in our sex life, shake things up a bit and keep him guessing what is next. I love to tease him every day. I will call him at work and say, "Hi, sexy. I want you to come home right after work. The kids are at their friends' tonight." Sometimes I put my panties in his lunch bag or brief-case or I flash him my breasts as he leaves in the morning. A few times I put a present from the sex-toy shop in our bed. Anything to put that shy-boy smile on his face.

DO YOU REMEMBER THE FIRST TIME YOU MASTURBATED?

The answers from those who responded ranged from men who said that they don't remember since they had been masturbating for as long as they could recall to women who hadn't masturbated until well into their thirties. I fall into that latter category.

What amazed me as I read the surveys was the depth of ignorance of most first-timers. Many freely admit that they had no idea what was happening. Sad, isn't it? I had a most enlightened mother for the mid-1950s when I was a teen. I was a curious kid and felt free to ask my mother any question at any time. So by the time I reached my early teens I knew the facts, at least. My attitudes were, of course, a product of the times and my mother's attitudes toward sex. I was fed the "company line" about masturbation being a no-no, that it just wasn't done. So I didn't touch myself for pleasure until I was in my thirties with two school-age children. Fortunately I was never told that my hands would fall off or that I would go blind, as I'm sure many males, and probably some females, were.

Parents, it's going to happen. Your sons, and probably your daughters, are going to masturbate. A bit of well-thought-through information will provide your children with truth and, during that discussion, you can also discuss some of your values.

A *thirty-one-year-old woman wrote:*

> I was seven. My first attempt at masturbation occurred rather by accident, but the end result was so pleasant that later that day I decided to try it again. Unfortunately, my mother walked into my bedroom and found me frantically rubbing between my legs and went ballistic. She convinced me that I would damage myself that way and have to have tubes put in to go to the bathroom. Needless to say I was terrified and it was years before I ever tried again.

What should you do if you stumble upon your child masturbating? First, and most important, take a deep breath before you decide how to handle it. Don't react with anger, embarrassment, or humiliation. Don't lie to your child as this parent did. If you do, he or she will never believe anything else you say, and you might be causing no end of sexual problems later on.

Temper any reaction with common sense and the reality of the letters you read here. Consider your views on sexuality and morality. Then explain to your child what's happening—that it's a normal bodily function—and physiologically why your child's body is reacting the way it is. If you just can't explain clearly (and that's too bad), get your child an age-appropriate book on sexuality and let him or her explore. If you're troubled by a child who masturbates at the dinner table, while watching TV, or in other public situations, suggest that masturbation is a very personal activity and that your child can do it (since he or she will do it anyway), but only in private. If you "go ballistic," as the parent did above, you'll risk making sex an unpleasant activity and severing all lines of communication.

It's really amazing how vivid the memories are for so many. Here's what others had to say about their first experience.

A *forty-two-year-old man wrote:*

> I was about twelve or thirteen. It was summer vacation and my

parents both worked, so I was home alone a lot. Some older boys had been showing a neighbor boy and me how to do it—by demonstrating, of course. I then tried to do the same but, since I didn't know what I was doing, I didn't "make it."

That night after I got into bed, I spontaneously came. It was very much like a wet dream, but I wasn't yet asleep.

By the next day I pretty much knew what was supposed to happen, so I really went at it, masturbating to orgasm several times. Of course, I told the neighbor boy right away and, proud of my new ability, I showed him.

Fairly soon he and I were doing it in each other's presence regularly. We did do each other, or at least tried, a few times, but having someone else jack me off wasn't as good as doing it myself. I remember that he was always harder to get off and, as I think back, I don't think I ever was able to bring him to orgasm. We never tried oral–penile contact on each other. Although we now live in separate towns, some distance apart, we're still good friends. I wonder whether he remembers that time as well as I do.

A sixty-two-year-old man wrote:

I was about twelve years old and I was with several other boys. It was a circle jerk in which we literally formed a circle and each boy massaged the penis of the boy next to him.

A sixty-eight-year-old man wrote:

Yes, I remember it well. I was twelve years old and was stroking my cock as I looked at drawings of female genitalia in my mother's anatomy book. Suddenly heaven(!) and huge jets of sperm.

A twenty-one-year-old woman wrote:

I remember the first time I masturbated. I was in my early teens, and scared to death that I was doing something evil. That didn't stop me, however, it just made me feel really guilty.

A forty-seven-year-old man wrote:

The first time I did it was about thirteen, in bed, thinking about Ms. V, my English teacher. A bunch of guys had been talking about sex for a while and somewhere in there I had started thinking of Ms. V's stockings. She must have been wearing thigh-highs and occasionally I could see her bare leg above the nylons. That first night I masturbated to that thought. After I came I wiped it off with a sock. Since my sister was in the other bed in the room, when I did it from then on I had to keep quiet, wait until she was asleep, and then do it.

A thirty-two-year-old man wrote:

I did it for the first time in the shower. I knew something was supposed to happen, but I ended up dropping to my knees due to the sensations. My mother thought I had fallen and killed myself. She never found out what had really happened.

A thirty-six-year-old woman wrote:

My first climax through sort-of masturbation happened by accident at the age of nineteen. I was really turned on by a dirty book I was reading. I had to use the bathroom and when I wiped with toilet paper after peeing I had an orgasm. I was mystified since I didn't know what was happening. I don't remember what I was thinking at that moment. I only remember my surprise when my body did things over which I had no control.

A twenty-six-year-old woman wrote:

The first time was after I had read a romance novel at age twelve. I was all tingly "down there" and began rubbing myself to soothe the "itch." Before I knew it I was having my first orgasm. Of course I didn't know what it was, but I knew it felt good.

A fifty-nine-year-old man wrote:

I was thirteen years old and ignorant. During that summer I was down in the basement where it was cool and I started playing with myself. It felt so good that I kept on until I came. The next day I tried it again, with no luck. I was probably really nervous about it all. Actually I don't remember the second time but I'll never forget that first.

A *twenty-year-old bisexual woman wrote*:

I don't remember my first time, but I do remember some of my early fantasies. Looking back, they were incredibly kinky for the twelve- to fourteen-year-old I was then. Lots of women in futuristic bondage, some sex-change stuff . . . and to think I didn't realize I was a kinky lesbianish bisexual till I was eighteen!

A *thirty-six-year-old woman wrote*:

The first time I masturbated I was eleven and had found my mother's book, *The Happy Hooker*, in her bedside table. I grabbed it and snuck it into my room.

The next afternoon, a warm summer day when everyone was busy outside, I hid myself in my bedroom. I got to the part in the book where she said that she had gotten off rubbing herself on the banister. I thought, *How is that possible?* I was quite horny by this time so I reached down between my legs and found that my panties were wet. With my fingers together and stiff, I rubbed hard like I imagined it would be like on a banister. Wow!! Holy shit it worked! I must have done that for the rest of the day. My mother had to call me three times for supper. I went to bed early that night, too.

A *twenty-eight-year-old man wrote*:

The first time I masturbated was by accident. I didn't know what masturbation or ejaculation were.

I was twelve years old and in my bedroom having just finished taking a bath. I had a towel around me and as I took it off to put my pajamas on, I noticed that my penis was stiff, bowed up in full erection as if begging to be touched. I remember sitting on

my bed and looking at it. I put my fingertips on the shaft and began stroking up and down very slowly. I felt a wave of excitement
as I continued to rub, and the more I stroked the better it felt. I
lay back on the bed and closed my eyes, feet on the floor, and
kept playing with myself as it felt better and better. It got to a
point where I could not believe how good it was when I suddenly felt a sensation like I was about to urinate. I let go of my
penis and watched in amazement as semen shot out.

My penis was throbbing and semen was still oozing as I
caught my breath. I told my mom about what happened and she
gave me a book about sex and masturbation, with pictures of
male and female genitalia. It taught me a lot, and I read the best
parts over and over when nobody was home.

A *twenty-two-year-old woman* wrote:

The first time I masturbated I was thirteen and I remember it
well. I had stayed home from school and, since my parents were
at work, I was alone for the entire day. My parents had a book by
Masters and Johnson about sex and I got it out and began reading about masturbation and intercourse. The book had a picture
of an erect penis and I got excited looking at it.

I removed my clothes and loved the way it felt as I walked
around the house naked. I gazed at my body in my mom's full-
length mirror, and remember looking at my breasts, swollen nipples, and my pubic hair. My body was almost all the way developed, and my nipples always seemed puffy, like they were still
growing. I got a mirror out and stared at my vulva. I pulled my clitoris hood back and looked at it, and I recall how good it felt as I
rubbed on it.

I spread my legs and began rubbing back and forth on the
hood of my clitoris, back and forth, back and forth. My clit felt hot
as I rubbed around it and on it. I went back and got the book and
looked at the erect-penis pictures, then pulled on my nipples as I
rubbed my vulva. I pulled lubrication to my clitoris area and the
slippery feeling of my fingers on my clit brought me only to the

edge of orgasm. I didn't climax until much later when I got better at stimulating myself.

The sex book was helpful in getting me excited for many masturbation sessions. The book described how the male penis gets erect, is inserted into the vagina, and, with a series of in-and-out movements, creates great physical pleasure for the male and female. I imagined how a penis would feel inside me as I rubbed my clitoris. This was how it all began for me at thirteen and I still masturbate with toys and my good old fingers sometimes.

A *twenty-seven-year-old woman* wrote:

The first time was when I was in high school. I had found some erotic magazines at my boyfriend's and borrowed them out of curiosity. I got so turned on looking at them that one thing led to another.

A *thirty-eight-year-old woman* wrote:

I was in fifth grade. I used to take baths at home, and we had a handheld hose that hooked onto the tub's spigot, supposedly to get all the soap out of my hair. The nozzle came off, leaving the open hose with water shooting out of it. I pointed it to my pussy and found my clit. I learned very early on what felt good, and would orgasm every time I took a bath.

A *twenty-six-year-old man* wrote:

The first time I masturbated I was thirteen. I was talking to an older woman on the phone and she talked me through it, slowly and gently. She told me that she was fingering herself as I stroked.

A *thirty-one-year-old man* wrote:

I actually remember two events. The first was the time I masturbated in the bathroom on a polar bear bath mat, not knowing exactly what I was doing. The second was when I was watching something on television, idly playing with myself, and I came. That time I finally knew what had happened.

A *thirty-two-year-old man wrote:*

I was about eleven years old and found a sex education book at a bookstore in a mall. It was pretty explicit, with photos. I got so aroused while reading it that I was actually rubbing my hard cock through my jeans right there in the store. Eventually I made myself come right there in the bookstore aisle. It was a little embarrassing trying to walk out of the mall with the obvious wet spot.

A *forty-five-year-old man wrote:*

Yes, I remember that first time distinctly. I felt like I'd just unwrapped the biggest present under the Christmas tree.

A *forty-seven-year-old man wrote:*

I was about twelve or so and when I found a box of condoms in my dad's nightstand I decided to try one on. Sliding the slippery latex tube on my penis felt so good that I just kept doing it over and over. On/off, up/down. I felt this strange sensation begin to build deep down in my loins. I thought maybe I should stop stroking, but it felt so good I just couldn't. Then suddenly *kaboom!* Huge waves of intense pleasure swept over me as I stared down in awe to see the condom fill up with white stuff.

A *twenty-one-year-old woman wrote:*

I was on the phone with my boyfriend and we had done cybersex before but I had *never* dared to put a finger in myself. That night proved to be most interesting.

A *twenty-five-year-old woman wrote:*

I don't remember exactly how old I was, but I was in elementary school. I was taking a bath and I lay on my back and let the water flow onto me until I climaxed. I didn't know what an orgasm was at the time, much less that I had just had one.

A *thirty-nine-year-old woman wrote:*

I was in my teens when I found out that, if I put a blanket or pillow between my legs, pressed my mound against it, and wiggled around, it created pleasurable feelings and eventually a release.

A *fifty-one-year-old man wrote:*

At age eleven I had not yet reached puberty but I did get little "boners." I started masturbating soon after those erections appeared but did not reach orgasm. As a matter of fact, I didn't know orgasms even existed. I just knew that it felt good.

At the start of summer when I was twelve I remember my friend Billy talking about being able to masturbate and he asked if I did. It sounded so manly that of course I said I did.

I had had zero sex education from my parents but I was too embarrassed to admit it to my friend or to admit that I didn't know what the hell I was doing when I did it. As so many boys did, I think Billy invited me over to his house to watch him. I went, and I remember being very tense and afraid. We ended up in the bathroom with me standing in the doorway—watching. He pulled down his pants, started playing with himself, and got this tiny erection, about three inches long. Well, he was off to the races, stroking very rapidly.

The first thing I noticed was we were the same size. See, even then size mattered. He held a coffee cup out in front of him and when he came I saw fluid squirt from his penis into the cup. He said he could do it all day and fill it up. I didn't know whether to believe him or not since I had never ejaculated myself, nor had I ever seen anyone else ejaculate. Then he turned to me and said, "Your turn."

I remember vividly just moving into the bathroom, dropping my pants and grabbing my cock, stroking myself more slowly than he had. I was scared to death, not knowing what would happen to my body. Suddenly I came for the first time. When I finally stopped, I looked up and there was his mother, hands on her hips, shouting at me to get out and never come back.

Caught, the very first time.

Boys talk and my best friend, Stevie, heard about all this from Billy. I remember from then on hating Billy so much I could have killed him. At first Stevie teased me, but then he asked me to go to his basement and do it with him.

So off we went to the basement where we dropped our drawers and masturbated together. The only thing I knew or cared about was that I liked it. We did this each day for about a week and then Stevie suggested we get naked and do it. I liked it even better this way. All my life, I have preferred to be naked during sex or masturbation. It makes a big difference for me.

At home, I would masturbate in the nude when I was alone or under my covers at night with my PJs stripped off. Then Stevie came up with the idea that he would put on his mom's bra and panties over his clothes and he had me lie down on top of him and hump away. Then we reversed the situation. That felt good, too, and we kept it up for a month: standing naked and masturbating or cross-dressing and humping each other. We eventually put the bra and panties on over our naked bodies, trading places each time. I remember liking our activities very much and looking forward to masturbating with him each day. At home I would think about what we had done that day and masturbate by myself.

Then one day Stevie wanted me to go to the woods with him and his friend Bob to masturbate together. Bob was six months older than we were and had already reached puberty. When we got to a secluded spot Bob told Stevie, "You might have to help me. Will you do it?" Stevie agreed. I had only seen small pre-puberty penises and when Bob pulled out this big fat cock, played with himself, and got this huge erection I was shocked and amazed.

I asked what Bob meant about helping so they showed me. Stevie knelt and started sucking Bob off and from the ease with which he did it I assume they had met in the woods often before. Finally Stevie challenged me to do it, but I wouldn't—I was afraid. Bob asked me to just touch it and I consented.

I touched the base of Bob's penis and pubic hair. I never felt anything like that before. When he told me to touch the knob, I rubbed his penis's head, then used both hands to stroke the top and bottom of his penis for a while longer. Bob continued stroking while Stevie rubbed his own penis and balls. When Bob ejaculated I was in shock. I saw this thick white come squirting two or three feet while he was moaning and groaning. We heard noises of people coming and left without me or Stevie climaxing.

Soon after that day, my family moved to a rural area where we had no neighbors and I made very few friends at school. I felt that this isolation was my punishment for my masturbation, and over the ensuing thirty-five years masturbation and sex were a source of guilt and shame for me. Sad, isn't it?

A thirty-five-year-old woman wrote:

I did it just a few years ago at my husband's urging, while we were making love. I have been hooked since.

A sixty-four-year-old man wrote:

The first time I recall masturbating was at about the age of ten or eleven. I was taking a bath and while soaking I discovered that if I touched my penis, it would pop up. I thought that was pretty neat so I spent a considerable amount of time making it pop up every time it went back down. Then I discovered something even better.

I found that if I made a tent of the washcloth so that it trapped a big bubble of air, brought it down under the water—under my penis and balls—and then squeezed the washcloth, a fine stream of bubbles would rise, tickling me. This not only made my penis pop up, but it felt really, really good. I was still too young to come and I had to stop when my mom wanted to know why I was taking so long in the tub.

three

LOVERS AND LOVEMAKING

Attraction, Confidence, Faking It, Positions,
the Most Unusual Place, the Wildest Thing,
the Most Recent, Wishes, Regrets

THE RESPONDENTS

B efore we get to more answers, I thought you'd be interested in some of the sexual habits of those who responded to my survey.

Of the men, 57% said they usually made love with the lights on, while only 39% of the women said they did. The majority of respondents preferred night-time trysts: 59% of the men and 52% of the women said that they usually made love at night. You know, making love in the morning is a great way to start the day, especially for men who have problems maintaining an erection. Testosterone levels are highest then. Where do people make love? Well, 80% of the men and 71% of the women said they usually did it in the bedroom. How sad. The rest of the house is so inviting. Have you ever noticed that the kitchen counters are just the right height for her to sit on and . . . ?

I asked whether the respondent ever wondered whether he or she was good at sex and if he or she had ever asked. Just over 62% of the men had wondered and 56% had asked. Of the women, 61% wondered but only 45% had asked. About 40% of men and women had told others they were good in bed even if they weren't.

I was not surprised that 60% of the women had faked orgasm—
but 42% of the men said they had faked it as well. That just blew
me away. I wished I had thought to ask why and how.

Okay, let's learn more about lovers and lovemaking.

WHAT IS YOUR FAVORITE POSITION DURING SEX?

In trying to answer this question myself, I realized that, for Ed and me, there is no one position. We move around a lot, and one position pretty much blends into another. We're comfortable with missionary, side to side, and a few that can't be described easily.

The folks who responded to my survey liked missionary, woman on top, and doggy-style most. Here are some of the answers they gave. Maybe you can get some new ideas.

A *twenty-one-year-old woman* wrote:

My favorite position is me on top of him, in control, sliding up and down on his erection. He likes me to be on top as well, but he also likes to have full penetration with him on top with my legs on his shoulders.

A *thirty-year-old woman* wrote:

I love doggy-style because he enters at an angle that's oh so good. Plus I like to be dominated in bed. He likes me on top but I don't like to be in control.

A *thirty-eight-year-old woman* wrote:

My favorite is me on top because my clit and my nipples can both be stimulated. We can make eye contact, too.

A forty-seven-year-old man wrote:

I like all kinds of positions. For the best orgasms for me I like to be on top or have her kneel before me and give me oral sex. I think she prefers being on top to bring her to climax.

A thirty-two-year-old man wrote:

My favorite is the woman on top, looking at me while we fuck, but I also like it when she is on top with her back to me. This allows me to use my fingers to massage her clitoris. Getting your hand there can be complicated, but I do like to please.

A thirty-six-year-old woman wrote:

I guess it depends on my mood. Mostly I like it with me on my back with my legs over my lover's shoulders—good eye contact and less weight. His favorite position is probably with me on my stomach and him on top entering my vagina from behind. He seems to orgasm best with me in this position.

A nineteen-year-old woman wrote:

Since the birth of my daughter my favorite position is being on the bottom because any other way still seems to hurt. Before having her, my favorite was doggy-style, and while I was pregnant it was the scissors position.

A twenty-six-year-old woman wrote:

We usually use the missionary position. If I hike my legs up high on his hips, I can usually achieve orgasm through his thrusting. He prefers doggy-style but I find it uncomfortable and rarely reach orgasm in this position.

A twenty-two-year-old man wrote:

My wife and I were experimenting with positions one night when we came across this absolutely excellent position that we use a lot now. The first time we used it, I was in absolute ecstasy.

Starting in the missionary position, my partner closed her legs to make her pussy really tight around my cock. At this point, I moved up into a seated position, so that I was sitting on her with my cock down, still inside her. I immediately felt the effects of this. She began to twist my nipples, and my body began to rock uncontrollably. She didn't even have to move. The sensations were so amazing that I couldn't stop myself. It felt like I came for ages, lasting longer than I had ever experienced.

A thirty-three-year-old woman wrote:

My fave is me on top. I don't know why but when I rock my pelvis it reaches my g-spot and the climax is so much better. His favorite is with me on all fours. Sometimes I like it but he's pretty big so sometimes I feel him too deep and it hurts.

A sixty-year-old man wrote:

I like all positions from time to time. For me having my partner sit on top is particularly exciting, because I can see her breasts dancing and all her body parts moving with her rhythm.

I also like entering her from behind with my lady on her elbows and knees. Maybe that is because it's a bit animal. Mostly I like to please the woman and let her choose the positions.

A fifty-nine-year-old man wrote:

I like it when my wife is on her left side with hips and knees slightly bent while I'm on my knees and come in from behind. I reach through her legs and grab her bottom (left) leg.

A twenty-year-old woman wrote:

I like my husband on top, doing most of the work (wicked grin). I love it when he pushes my legs over my head, getting really deep penetration.

He seems to like me on top, or us side by side, but he has a definite aversion to the classic missionary position. I don't mind side by side, though I find it a little boring. Me on top is okay for a short while, until my muscles start screaming at me.

A *twenty-one-year-old man* wrote:

I like it when we're both sitting on the floor and she puts her legs on the outside of mine.

A *thirty-one-year-old man* wrote:

I like it best when I take her from behind. I love to watch my cock sink into her, and I love the feel of her ass as it hits my hips when we fuck. I'm an ass lover so I love to grind into hers.

A *forty-seven-year-old woman* wrote:

Any position is fine with me, I love them all, but I really enjoy my lover on top of me, so I can watch his face. It is so beautiful seeing his expressions, like he is playing a fine instrument, so intense.

My husband loves all positions, but he says that he really loves me on top of him, because he can watch me "ride" him and watch my beautiful breasts, as our bodies connect and become one. He says that he loves watching me because I show so much love for him and his body. He also loves being on top of me so he can kiss me often while we make love. He never grows tired of kissing me, nor I him.

A *twenty-six-year-old woman* wrote:

I like sitting on top, then moving to missionary position. Missionary allows deeper penetration and a feeling of closeness you don't get from other positions. In addition, I like looking at my partner's face during sex. I will also admit that I'm kind of lazy sometimes, and missionary means I don't have to do as much work.

A *thirty-one-year-old man* wrote:

I really enjoy when she is standing in front of me, facing away, and bends over to grab her ankles as I enter her vaginally from behind. She prefers if I'm lying on my back with her sitting on top of me so that she can control the angle, depth, and speed with which I enter her. I enjoy that, too, but she goes too damn fast.

A twenty-three-year-old woman wrote:

I love when he is on top and my legs are on his chest. When he gets pumping really good he hits the right spot. I love doggy-style when I just want to be fucked. He likes it when I'm on top, the whole female domination thing, and the fact that he doesn't have to work very hard.

A twenty-seven-year-old woman wrote:

I love to lie on my side, with him straddling my bottom leg, holding my top leg against his chest as he enters me. He prefers to enter me from behind, while standing up. I would like it more if it wasn't the only way he'd have sex with me anymore.

A twenty-eight-year-old woman wrote:

My favorite position is me on top so my back is toward him and I am looking at his feet. That way I can play with his balls and we can both play a little in the anal area—plus it's a great view for me.

A thirty-year-old woman wrote:

I have three. I lie on my back with my head hanging a little off the side of the bed. The guy stands or kneels in front of me so that I can perform oral sex. This leaves my body completely open for him to watch, touch, or sixty-nine.

The next one is also for oral sex. We lie on our sides in a sixty-nine position and I perform oral sex, and at the same time, masturbate so that he can watch. It is a very up-close view.

The third position works well for orgasm for me. After the guy ejaculates in the missionary position, he stays inside me and does not move. I slowly move my hips up, down, and around until I have an orgasm. It's important that he stay totally still.

A *thirty-one-year-old woman* wrote:

Doggy-style. And it's even better if my hands are tied to the headboard.

A *thirty-eight-year-old woman* wrote:

My favorite position is to lie on my back, my shoulders flat on the bed. Then I twist at the waist so my knees are together on the left side of me, and my partner enters me kind of sideways. It hits a spot inside me unlike any other. It's not the most natural position, and it's not the easiest to maintain, but it sure does work!

A *forty-one-year-old woman* wrote:

We both like making love on our sides facing each other with legs intertwined. It is comfortable and easy.

A *forty-two-year-old woman* wrote:

I like the spoon position because the penetration is great and I love the closeness.

A *forty-three-year-old woman* wrote:

I like it with him on top and me on bottom so he can suck and bite my nipples.

A *forty-five-year-old woman* wrote:

Years ago, one of my lovers liked me to lie on my back, legs wide apart, with his hands holding my ankles out wide to the side. I liked it because of the deep penetration, and because I could reach down and feel him pumping in and out of me. I could also diddle my clit to orgasm. I must admit, however, the older I get, the less I like this position. I'm not that flexible anymore.

A *twenty-seven-year-old woman* wrote:

If I'm tired, I like the spoon position with him behind me. During a visit to my ob-gyn I was told it would be easier for me to conceive that way and it has become a favorite because of how easily he can touch me. The drawback is I can't see or touch him.

A *fifty-eight-year-old woman wrote:*

Hmmm, how do I count the ways? I think it isn't the position, but the partner, but if I had to choose, I'd say having him seated and me on top, facing him, is the best. It lets me control the rhythm, speed, depth, while his mouth is in close proximity to my breasts, and his strong hands are clutching my ass. And, of course, it lets him control our movements if the spirit moves him. I like it because we have eye contact, he's comfortable, and I can reach climax after climax by the deep penetration and letting my clit rub against his body.

He likes it when he can take me from behind, at an angle that doesn't hurt his back. He can pump deep inside me and drive me wild. He also likes it when he positions me with my ass on the edge of his bed so he can enter me while he's standing, holding my legs high and spread. That way he can control our movements. Sometimes he'll raise my ass off the bed and hook my legs over his shoulders so he can suck me, which drives me crazy.

Like all things, variety is the spice of life, so I like to try new positions. I love the ones I know bring him pleasure, just as he seems to love the ones that bring me pleasure.

A *thirty-two-year-old man wrote:*

I like having my wife on top so I can suck on her sexy, hard nipples and watch her face as she reaches orgasm. I also like to have her kneel facedown on the side of the bed so I can stand and enter her from behind. I get excited as I watch my cock sliding in and out as her pussy lips cling to me. I sometimes slide a lubed finger into her ass and she goes absolutely wild.

A *thirty-six-year-old man wrote:*

Doggy-style is the best for me, with my left hand around my cock so I can stroke her clit and my right hand on her back with my thumb rubbing her rectum. She is never more vocal!

A *forty-year-old man wrote*:

We both like the missionary position with my wife's head and shoulders jacked up with pillows so that she can see the workings of our respective parts.

A *forty-two-year-old man wrote*:

I guess my personal favorite is lying on my side with her on her back, with one leg over me and her other leg between mine. It gives good access to her clitty and allows me to take my time, while not being tiring at all.

A *forty-two-year-old man wrote*:

My wife likes to come again afterward by lying on her side, facing me, squeezing her legs together and rubbing her clit while I hold her ass cheeks as firmly as I can. Sometimes she asks me to finger her ass.

A *sixty-eight-year-old man wrote*:

There are many, but I love to come kneeling behind a woman who has already come, and is wide open because of it. I love to hold her ass cheeks and pull her back on my cock as I climax. The failing here is that I can't see her eyes as she comes.

A *twenty-five-year-old woman wrote*:

I like it when I'm lying on my stomach, legs slightly apart at first, and he enters me from behind. Once his cock is inside me I close my legs and hold them tightly together. When he thrusts it's one of the best sensations.

A *fifty-five-year-old man wrote*:

Due to my wife's back problems, this is our favorite. She lies on her back and I lie on my right side, perpendicular to her. She raises her left leg, and I enter her under that leg. Great for clitoral tension.

A sixty-two-year-old man wrote:

For pure self-indulgence, I like my partner to rub me down, then work on my penis and balls, gently and slowly taking me up and down the emotional scale until I am begging for her mouth. When she takes me in and strokes my anus (or better, puts her finger in) I am *gone!*

She likes it when I gently massage her while she's lying on her tummy, then work into her pussy area, massaging her outer lips between thumb and finger, rubbing her clit with little flicks. Then she turns over for me to suck her nipples while massaging her pussy and slowly inserting my finger into her anus. Finally, over and up for a dog-style screw, sometimes with a finger in her anus if she wants it.

A fifty-six-year-old man summed it all up. He wrote:

Do I have a favorite position? Sure. The one I am in! I have not found that one position is better than another. They are all great!

WHAT IS THE MOST UNUSUAL PLACE YOU'VE EVER MADE LOVE?

Some of the best stories I got were in answer to this question. In several cases I wanted to write back and ask for more details. I would have loved the full story to "On the ice at the hockey rink," or "In a horse stall," or "On top of the dishwasher on Christmas Day," or "On the top of my kids' bunk beds," but alas, I didn't want to embarrass anyone. And how did the twenty-eight-year-old woman and her boyfriend make out on the hood of a police car in a field in a public park? Hmmm.

Are all these stories true? I don't know, but they're so delicious that I'm not going to worry about it. Many tell similar tales, but the differences are in the people involved and their reactions.

In my case, the most unusual place I ever made love involved a long-ago boyfriend who was hospitalized for hepatitis, which, by the way, he shared with me. Anyway, we were new to the relation-ship so we were both hungry most of the time. After three long days of visiting him we finally got so hot that we did it in the room's small bathroom with me leaning against the sink and him behind, both of us watching in the mirror. I think wondering whether some nurse might walk in on us added to the excitement. Oh yes, he was in a private room.

I've also made love in a hot tub, or tried to. My guy at the time found the hot water really exciting mentally, but debilitating physically. Let's just say the spirit was willing but the flesh was flaccid.

Oh, and have you ever noticed that your dining room table is just the right height? Mine is.

Let's see what those who responded to the survey wrote.

A thirty-two-year-old woman wrote:

We were with friends camping and everyone went for a midnight swim. When the camp owner heard all the noise she made everyone else leave, but my wife and I had swum off to the rocks near the shore so she didn't see us. When the lady went back inside, we removed our suits, swam back out to the middle of the lake, and made love on the swim float, under the stars, in plain view of the entire campsite.

A fifty-four-year-old man had more success in a hot tub than I did. He wrote:

My wife and I made love in a hot tub at a resort up north. We were both naked and it was more foreplay than we usually indulged in. We were playing, trying to get off on the water jet. My wife actually had an orgasm, then used her hands to get me off too.

A nineteen-year-old woman wrote:

This guy I was dating and I did it on a weight bench in his parents' shed. We were really horny and that was the only place that we could find. The bench was very narrow, but we managed.

A forty-eight-year-old man wrote:

My wife had dragged me to Nordstrom's to shop and while she was looking at lingerie, I was looking at her. Let me just say that we found a back staircase and, well . . . we didn't actually have intercourse, but we both climaxed from some really heavy petting.

A twenty-two-year-old man wrote:

A girl I dated many years ago and I actually did it on a bench in a nearby park. It was my first outdoor experience with anyone, so I was quite scared. She got totally naked but I just got my cock out because I was worried about being seen. She was making really loud noses, and I kept telling her to be quieter or we'd get caught. Maybe she got off on the danger, and maybe she just wanted to embarrass me, but she wouldn't quit the noise.

When she came, she screamed, "YES!!!!! FUCK ME!!!" really loud. I was petrified.

A thirty-three-year-old woman wrote:

My then-boyfriend and I were taking a walk near his parents' house, which is very out of the way. We held hands and started talking about sex. I asked him about his fantasies and he said that he'd really enjoy taking me while I leaned against a tree. The idea really turned me on so I told him I was game. He looked up, surprised, since I was, at that time, very prudish about sex.

So . . . I found a suitable tree and was already getting wet just thinking about it. I had snaps on my pant legs so I just pulled them open. The cold air struck my hot parts but it was not un-pleasant . . . it even felt pretty nice. He started to pet me but I grabbed him and made him understand that I wanted to be pen-etrated . . . which he did. I completely lost it! The environment, the fact that we were pretty much dressed and that we could get caught got me to a very intense climax.

A sixty-year-old man wrote:

I've done it in several unusual places, but I guess the oddest was on a beach under a blanket, with a lot of people lying around us. It was really chilly and windy and I had cuddled behind my wife, completely covered by the blanket. People could not see me; they just saw her, lying on her side, covered with a blanket from shoulders to toes, reading a book. It all looked perfectly innocent, except that her entire body, including her large breasts, was moving with my fucking rhythm. Now and then she looked up, glanced around, and smiled at people near us.

Later she told me that one man sitting there with his wife and three children seemed to know what was going on and kept looking at her, watching her bobbing breasts and body. When he could hardly stand up anymore because of the erection in his swimming trunks, he left the kiddies and lured his wife into their bungalow. A great afternoon for all of us.

A fifty-nine-year-old man wrote:

It's not the unusual things I've done that stick out in my mind, but the unusual places I've done them. My wife and I really enjoy great sex and we find we're horny most of the time. Therefore . . .

1. On an island in the San Juans one sunny day on a gentle, wild-strawberry–covered hillside. Bright blue sky, puffy white clouds, the sound of a nearby horse, and all afternoon to make love.

2. Next to the railroad tracks in northern California on our way to Reno. Between I-5 and Susanville, we pulled off next to a major manzanita stand, grabbed the blanket, and walked a short way into the pines. The sun was warm but the air was cool, and there were patches of snow about. We found a place in the sun that was out of the wind but only twenty feet from the railroad tracks. We had a quickie and, just as we were finishing, along came a passenger train. Any of the people on the train who happened to glance our way knew what was going on.

3. In the backyard on a warm summer night. We put the pad from our lounge chair on the grass and just got started. Both of our cats came to join us. We started laughing so hard we had to go inside to finish our fun.

4. We've also done it quite a few times in the car. Once we made love in the backseat of our Camaro and once we did it just to break in the new Olds. I remember one particular af-

ternoon alongside I-15 in Montana. The sun was bright but the air outside was freezing. We left the engine on, turned up the heater, and fogged up the windows something fierce. Ain't it great!

A forty-seven-year-old man wrote:

I once got a blow job in a Victoria's Secret dressing room. There was only one salesclerk in a smaller store along the boardwalk in Atlantic City. We were on the second floor and a couple of customers were keeping the salesgirl busy downstairs. My wife was in the dressing room trying on some stuff and, when I realized we were alone, I took advantage and slipped into the dressing stall. My wife blew me and it was unbelievable. As I left the dressing room the girls were coming up the stairs and they saw me leave it. I think they knew but they just smiled.

Another time my wife and I made love in our hotel room in New York with the shades open. It was sort of an impromptu act one night when we returned from the theater. We had been going at it for more than an hour, and she had come several times, but I hadn't. She was lying there with me on top of her, our heads toward the window. I happened to look out and was shocked to see a couple in the office tower next door looking at us.

After overcoming my shock (which must not have been much since my cock grew still harder) I pulled out and straddled my wife. I put my cock in her face and she began sucking. I have to tell you I had to hold back. I wanted to come right away but I wanted to give a good show, too!

Anyway, I fucked my wife's face for a while, glancing from time to time at the couple in the other building, seeing them but not acknowledging them. My wife grabbed my ass and pulled me into her mouth, building me up for the big event, and finally I came, first in her mouth, then pulling out and spattering her face. It was awesome! She pulled my dick back into her mouth and she cleaned it off, keeping me hard. I slid back inside her pussy to give her what she called later a delicious orgasm. When I finally looked up again, the blinds were drawn in the office window. I wonder what they were doing! (Grinning)

A *thirty-three-year-old woman wrote*:

One day we made it in the backyard in the rain. It was with my ex-fiancé, but what made it so fantastic is that he performed oral sex on me, almost bringing me to orgasm that way before we actually fucked. There we were, outside in the rain for all to see. Nobody did ... that I know of, but it was the most romantic sexual event of my life.

A *forty-seven-year-old woman wrote*:

I remember the night my boyfriend and I made love up against the wall inside a machine shop where he worked. All the smells of grease and coveralls, ohhhhhh, it was heavenly. It might seem strange to you but all those cold, shiny machines and the smell of grease really turned me on.

A *thirty-six-year-old woman wrote*:

Unusual? Well, the only time I made love in public was at my parents' house many years ago during a family Thanksgiving gathering. Hubby and I were on the floor in the family room under an old bulky sleeping bag watching TV and talking. The sex was okay and my husband got off. I was not comfortable about it, though, thinking, *Oh my, my father is looking.* He wasn't but he could have been.

A *thirty-one-year-old man wrote*:

We once made love in a small boat in the middle of the Lake of the Ozarks. It was close to sunset and my wife and I were feeling a bit daring, so we stopped and made love while the sun went down.

A *twenty-two-year-old woman wrote*:

I've made love in lots of unusual places. I have had sex on a pool table that wasn't mine, on the beach, in a car in a wheat field, on the dryer, and on the bathroom counter.

A *twenty-three-year-old woman* wrote:

I hadn't seen my husband in a long time so, when I went to visit him while he was on military duty, we actually made it in the back of an army tactical vehicle. The short version of the story is that we just snuck in past the guard on duty, climbed in the back of the Hummer, and fucked like rabbits.

A *twenty-five-year-old woman* wrote:

I can't believe we did this and I can't believe I'm telling you about it. We were both very young and very dumb and very horny. We were at the lake at the beginning of January. It was unseasonably warm, but still cold, and it was raining to boot. My husband and I got adventurous and climbed out of our truck and up on the hood. Yes, we did it at the lake on the hood of a '76 Dodge Power Wagon in the rain in January. Oh, and we both got sick from that one.

A *twenty-seven-year-old woman* wrote:

The most unusual place would have to be on top of a railroad car. We were teenagers and out for a walk along a road that wound along the train tracks that led out of town. It was a beautiful, romantic night with a full moon and my honey and I were in the mood to play. We were with some other people, so we ducked around the train, lost them, then climbed on top of the car and fucked. It was wonderful. Being completely naked, spiced with the chance that we might get caught, made for one erotic night.

A *thirty-year-old woman* wrote:

I guess the most unusual and romantic night was one beautiful summer evening on my apartment's patio. Since we don't care to be exhibitionist my boyfriend and I hung a blanket around the railing and made love outside. It was very nice: moonlight, a soft breeze, and the music of my neighbor's wind chimes. Although it was many years ago, I specifically remember that after he kissed my neck or anywhere else for that matter the slight wind would hit that damp spot. It felt wonderful.

A thirty-one-year-old woman wrote:

You might not believe me but I've actually made love on the football field at Mississippi State University—in the off season of course. My ex-boyfriend and I climbed a fence late one night—both absolutely plastered—and did our thing on the fifty-yard line. We ran into a security guard on our way out and feigned innocence, but I could tell by the grin on his face as he inspected the grass stains on our clothes that he knew just what we had been up to!

A thirty-five-year-old woman wrote:

We did it in the middle of the woods in broad daylight. We were out mushroom hunting and I got bored so I told hubby I had to take a pee stop. I dropped my pants behind a tree, bent over touching the ground, and softly called his name. Of course he couldn't resist temptation, and we had hard pounding sex in the middle of the woods, not caring that others could be in there and see us.

A thirty-eight-year-old woman wrote:

I did it on a catwalk over a theater. Many years ago I had an affair with a man I worked with who was a sound engineer and had access to all kinds of places behind the scenes. One day he took me to the top of a stairwell and opened a door that took us onto the catwalk above a busy theater. The crew was setting up stage below us, the colored lights were on, and the rock and roll was very loud with heavy bass pounding everywhere. He bent me over a rail and lifted my skirt, entering me from behind. The act lasted several minutes, and being the oral kind of person I am, I was yelling my fool head off, unbeknownst (I think) to all the people below us. It was incredibly erotic knowing that we could be seen, and it was dangerous because we could have actually fallen off the catwalk. I'll never forget that time, and neither will he.

A forty-two-year-old woman wrote:

My husband Ron and I once made love in a van parked behind McCormick Place in downtown Chicago, and let me tell you it was great. After the deed was done we fell asleep naked. Some time later I felt a light in my eyes and looked out the front window. You guessed it, it was a cop. I was so startled that I jumped up and, of course, the cop saw me in all my glory. The cop just stood there as we started the engine and hotfooted it out of there. Later Ron and I drove down Lake Shore Drive in our birthday suits, laughing like crazy.

A forty-three-year-old woman wrote:

I guess the swimming pool was the most unusual place my husband and I ever did it. Our pool was in the back of our property where there was some privacy but we could have been caught. My husband was feeling frisky and made me sit on the ladder while he ate my pussy right out there in the open where anyone could have walked up and caught us. I found it very hard to relax but was able to climax. If anyone saw us, I really do not want to know.

A forty-seven-year-old woman wrote:

We did it at a family picnic in full view of our relatives—sort of. We had put our baby down in an upstairs bedroom and he had just fallen asleep. Someone called from the backyard to ask when we were coming down, and I leaned out the window and called that we would be out in a few minutes. All this time my husband was kneeling behind me with his fingers and tongue working.

At that moment my husband stood up, peered over my shoulder, and started talking to them, too, raising his voice to be heard. Still talking, he moved my panties aside and entered me. He continued to move in and out slowly while people below were just walking around. He had one arm around my shoulder like he was just standing behind me.

I was getting a little nervous and a lot turned on what with doing it in full view of my relatives, and I finally told him to stop. Needless to say, he didn't. I was afraid someone would look up and realize what was going on, but finally it got to the point where I didn't care. We both came at the same time, fortunately reasonably quietly.

A *fifty-one-year-old woman* wrote:

My husband knew that I had a fantasy about making love outside and one day he was so sweet that he made it happen. We went to an out-of-the-way place on a bluff above the ocean, a beautiful spot with old pine trees and pine-needle–softened ground. He had brought a big thick blanket and we made love under the trees. It was so beautiful and I loved him for that, especially since I knew it wasn't something he was really anxious to do.

A *twenty-five-year-old man* wrote:

Does a dryer qualify as an unusual place? It was with my first lover and we did it with her bent over the dryer. Man did she love it that way. She would move her ass in such a way that it seemed my cock was turning in circles within her. Talk about fireworks.

A *twenty-seven-year-old man* wrote:

The most bizarre place I ever did it was in a girlfriend's dorm room, secretly, while her exchange-student roomie did her homework. It began with us just cuddling under the covers but it kept getting more intense. Eventually it turned into a tease game where she'd stroke my cock and I'd tease her nipples and clit, all very hush-hush. We got ourselves so hot that we finally couldn't help it. We fucked slow and easy, controlling our voices. Did the roomie know? Probably, but she never told. How hot is that!!!

A thirty-one-year-old man wrote:

How about a mall stairway? A then-girlfriend and I had gotten together in the middle of the day, and she'd brought a bottle of
vodka. By the time we got to the mall, we were both toasted.
She kept grabbing my dick and being loud and rowdy. It was kind
of embarrassing, and I told her that she'd better knock it off or I
was going to take her up on it. She taunted again so we went off
in search of a place. We found the door to the employee stairs
and slipped inside. She gave me a fabulous blow job and then
we had no-"holes"-barred sex.

A thirty-two-year-old man wrote:

About four years ago my wife and I attended the wedding of
one of her friends. The reception was in a hotel banquet room
with a large outdoor patio. My wife and I were teasing each
other on the dance floor, and pointing out other sexy-looking
people to each other.

After a particularly steamy slow dance, my wife grabbed me
by the hand and pulled me out on the patio, where there were
about five other couples enjoying the fresh air. She dragged me
into a corner that was not immediately visible to anyone unless
they actually made the effort to look.

She proceeded to kneel in front of me, pull down my zipper,
and gently reach inside for my now rock-hard shaft. It was oozing
so much that it had made a wet spot on the front of my pants.
She had a devilish look in her eyes as she stuck her tongue out
to lick the entire length, before she took almost my entire cock in
her mouth and slowly sucked me in. As we were in a risky situation, she didn't treat me to one of her usual torturously slow
blow jobs. As soon as she had me in her mouth she started bobbing up and down, faster and faster.

As I looked around to make sure no one came up to us, I noticed a couple in the building across the alley. The woman
stopped and pointed us out to her partner. I didn't tell my wife,

afraid she would stop, but I became even more excited watching the voyeuristic couple grope each other while staring at us. My wife was going faster and using her hand along with her mouth, and although I wanted to make it last for our peeping companions, I was getting too close to orgasm to stop. In no time at all I signaled my wife that I was ready to come, so she moved aside and jerked me off. I erupted over the side of the railing and onto the street below. My wife then saw the other couple and just smiled and waved, while I tried to get my still-hard cock back in my pants.

A thirty-two-year-old man wrote:

It's amazing what a pair of horny high school students without any regular place to make out will do. This girl and I did it on the roof of a four-story office complex where I was doing some contractual janitorial work. We went at it in broad daylight, in the middle of the day.

A thirty-six-year-old man wrote:

I met a woman one night in a community park and we started making out in the car. We couldn't get comfortable so we walked over to the jungle gym. We were up there, neither with any pants on, when the police came and broke it up. Luckily the cop just told us to leave, with a grin.

A thirty-nine-year-old man wrote:

My wife and I made out once in the bathroom while she sat on the edge of the sink. It was just passionate fucking. The funny thing was that when she came she leaned on her hand and squeezed the tube of toothpaste all over her ass. We still laugh about that.

A forty-five-year-old man wrote:

The university in our town has a conference center built around a lovely old house and a friend had her wedding reception there.

All the food and entertainment was on the main floor, but the washrooms were all on the second level. I realized with a little exploring during a trip up there that there were a number of smaller meeting and lounge rooms, at least one of which had a door that locked from the inside.

It was one of those hot-as-hell summer evenings and the center wasn't air-conditioned. The heat, plus all the skimpy summer dresses, were making me as horny as hell. Finally I was able to get my wife to go upstairs to use the facilities. When she came out of the bathroom there was no one else around so I took her by the arm and led her down this dimly lit hallway to a room at the end. I'm not sure that she knew what I wanted when I closed and locked the door behind us, but when I started kissing her and pulling her dress off she got the idea. It certainly wasn't a prolonged encounter but it was a dynamite experience. I think we probably looked a little flushed and sweaty when we returned to the main floor but no one seemed to notice. What's even more exciting is thinking that maybe we weren't the only ones to do the same thing that night.

A forty-eight-year-old man wrote:

My current lover has a hot tub, and right after we started making it regularly, we were in her hot tub and she initiated sex by climbing right into my lap. We went at it with her sitting on my crotch, facing me. It was really pretty good as her weight was counterbalanced by the water and I could get my fingers onto her clitty pretty well. I just kept playing with it until she came. The combined motion and the feeling of her cunt squeezing my penis brought me off just a moment later.

We've never done it that way again because she said she had to change the water. I guess I probably should have worn a condom because she told me she didn't like come in it. All in all, I'd rate that particular session as one of our best, but I don't know if she'd say the same.

A fifty-six-year-old man wrote:

One of the first times my then-girlfriend and I made love was one of the first times we spent a night at her house. We had been tantalizing each other sensuously and sexually all evening, bringing each other to higher and higher levels of sexual tension.

I was only wearing a dress shirt and she had put on one of my other ones before going into the kitchen to refill our wineglasses. Not really enjoying being away from her for a minute, added to the fact that she has great legs, I followed her. Of course I kissed her and my hands wandered to her legs and her gorgeous ass, and eventually to her incredibly sexy pussy. I kissed her and played with her pussy lips until she was virtually dripping and my fingers entered her deeper and deeper with little effort. We kissed and played with my hand inside her pussy until she had a very strong orgasm. Strange, but I didn't need to come right then—her climax was so good for me, too.

A seventy-seven-year-old man wrote:

We made love on the beach one evening at twilight. It was made more delicious for us because we could hear people on the boardwalk above as they discussed the moon rising over the ocean. I think we would have quite literally died if anyone had seen us.

A twenty-five-year-old woman wrote:

My ex-husband and I were walking in the park, thinking about how quiet and secluded it was. We thought about doing it right there, and were sort of anxious about getting caught. That made it all the sexier.

I started by performing oral sex on him while he stood over me. He stopped me before he came and told me to lower my pants. I was nervous but complied with his delicious "demand." I lowered my jeans and panties and he began to run his fingers over my wetness, slowly inserting a finger and teasing me with a mock fuck. Then he told me to turn around and lean forward. He moved behind me and inserted his penis in me. He grabbed me by the waist, occasionally telling me to arch my back this way, move my behind that way so that he could thrust more deeply. He reached under and rubbed my clit while he thrust still harder. Unfortunately he didn't bring me to climax but it was still good.

A twenty-five-year-old woman wrote:

Before my fiancé and I were living together, he was staying with a friend. There was only one bathroom for the whole apartment building. We'd go in there every chance we got and make love. When my friend kept asking us if we were sick, we just giggled.

A thirty-year-old woman wrote:

We did it outside in the yard. We climbed out the window and got all dirty—it was raining—but we giggled and did it right there. Then we went into the shower with our clothes on and did it again.

A thirty-nine-year-old woman wrote:

I don't know if this is unusual, but it was the most public place I've ever made love. My partner and I were vacationing in the Ozarks, staying at a local motel, and we went swimming late one evening. My partner knew how to turn me on and he teased me until I was ready for anything. We moved to the shallow end of the pool while he caressed my breasts and buttocks and kissed me behind my ears and along my neck. He pulled aside my swimsuit panties, pulled his cock out over his swim trunks, and entered me. He kissed me on the mouth to silence my moans so we didn't attract attention. Just as we finished, a couple came out of their room. Did they see us and watch for a while? Who knows?

A fifty-five-year-old man wrote:

We did it in our first recliner. I was sitting in it, nude, when my wife decided to get frisky. When I was hard as a rock, she sat down on my cock and I held on for dear life. It was amazing, but the chair almost broke. We did it there often but when we moved we had to give up the old, worn chair. We watched as the garbagemen picked it up, along with all our delicious memories.

A sixty-two-year-old man wrote:

My wife and I made love in a fancy hotel in Coconut Grove, Florida. Our bed was on a raised dais with lighting and music controls in the headboard, and mirrors all around. There was also a big bath with all the trimmings, including a selection of oils, candles—everything to make your fantasy dreams come true. We had a fantastic time, making love twice that night, and twice again in the morning. Recently we wanted to go back but we discovered that the hotel is closed. Too bad!

A sixty-nine-year-old man wrote:

My lady and I made love on a sailboat. We thought the boat was securely tied to the dock, but it must have come loose. It drifted along on the current, past the front of a hotel full of guests who were all watching our action.

A forty-seven-year-old man wrote:

My best sex ever was with my second full-time partner. Location, location, location was what made sex with her so much fun. We did it everywhere: in a horse stall, a car, outdoors on a pool slide, in the pool, in the changing room next to the pool, and at the community college where I worked. We even did it in bed once or twice.

WHAT WAS THE WILDEST THING YOU EVER DID WHILE MAKING LOVE?

I do like the attitude of the people who answered that they hadn't done anything wild—yet. And I particularly admire the twenty-seven-year-old woman who wrote:

> I have tried most things, from water sports to BDSM, from foods to candles and groups. If It Feels Right, Go Ahead is my motto.

Bravo!!!

A thirty-two-year-old man wrote:

> One night I surprised my wife with a little light bondage. I gently tied her arms and legs to the bedpost, massaged and teased her, then made oral love to her with a little added surprise. I had bought our first dildo and I experimented, knowing she would tell me if I did anything wrong. I guess I did okay, since she came twice. Sadly, this was the first and last time that happened, so far.

I can't help but wonder why they haven't done this again.

A forty-eight-year-old man wrote:

> The wildest thing I ever did was get spanked during sex. I don't

know quite how it happened but while I was fucking an old girl-friend of mine, she just reached around and slapped my ass. I came right then with one of the most outrageous orgasms of my life. She and I didn't work out and never made love again. I've been too embarrassed to suggest it to any girl since.

A *twenty-two-year-old man* wrote:

Probably the wildest was recently when, while I was having sex with her, my girl asked me to be really aggressive and call her names. I found it very difficult to begin with, but eventually I got really into it. When I called her a slut she came so hard that she almost bounced me out of bed. I'm still getting into it but she's the greatest, so I'm trying.

A *thirty-eight-year-old man* wrote:

The wildest was when I slipped a dildo in my lover's ass while screwing her. She went ballistic.

A *twenty-year-old bisexual woman* wrote:

Probably the wildest has been a couple of kinky threesomes. My previous girlfriend and I once got together with a man who was into S&M. That was a really interesting evening. He attached pairs of nipple clamps from her to me while we were bound. We couldn't move without tugging on each other's nipples. Evil in a nice way.

The ludicrously huge butt plug was quite entertaining as well. I had seen it the night before on his windowsill and went, "Bloody hell, is that a butt plug?" It was the size of my hand! The next morning, I ended up on my hands and knees with something I couldn't see being applied to my bottom. "That's not . . . not the butt plug from the windowsill, is it?" I asked. My girlfriend and our male friend giggled evilly and I shivered in terror. In his expert hands, however, it slipped in incredibly easily (even he was sur-prised) and life has not been quite the same since. After you've had something the size of a small flowerpot up your bottom, things look kind of different.

A *thirty-three-year-old woman wrote:*

Maybe it was doing it during dinner at a restaurant. I was able to bring my partner to orgasm by jerking him off under the table. The best part about it was that the waitress knew what I was doing. At one point she caught my eye and winked.

A *twenty-one-year-old man wrote:*

The wildest thing that ever happened was when I handcuffed my girl to the bed and teased her for a good half an hour to the point where she broke down and just kept coming. Then I untied her and we fucked in every room of the house.

A *fifty-one-year-old woman wrote:*

It was the first time I asked him to spank me, erotically, not so it hurts—too much. Now I love to be slapped on my ass, especially during anal sex.

A *forty-seven-year-old woman wrote:*

Despite all the jokes I squirted whipped cream all over my lover, head to toe, and then I licked it all off inch by inch.

A *thirty-one-year-old man wrote:*

In college I dated a girl who liked to be tied up. One time I tied her in a kneeling position and put a small remote-control vibrating egg inside her. Then I had her take me in her mouth and suck me *very* slowly. As long as she was doing a good job and going slowly enough I would let the egg vibrate at varying speeds. If she stopped or went too fast, I'd turn it off. By the time I finished with her she had had half a dozen orgasms. We were both so exhausted that when I untied her she and I immediately crawled into bed for a long nap.

A *twenty-five-year-old woman wrote:*

My husband and I were both intoxicated and playing with our

toys. One time I took a dildo, lubed it up, and stuck it up his butt. Then I climbed on his dick and rode him. He didn't last long and I got filled wfth his come.

A *thirty-one-year-old woman wrote:*

I fulfilled one of my husband's fantasies. I jerked him off between my breasts until he came all over my face, and then spent minutes massaging his cum into my neck and breasts. He loved it.

A *thirty-four-year-old woman wrote:*

Lots of kissing, foreplay, and oral sex—but no intercourse. With two guys at the same time. Fabulous!

A *forty-seven-year-old woman wrote:*

Wild? Well I like chocolate on my husband's penis, and he says grapes are nice when hidden you-know-where.

A *fifty-one-year-old woman wrote:*

Possibly holding an ice cube in my mouth as I sucked him. Or being bent over the arm of the sofa in the living room for anal sex.

A *twenty-seven-year-old man wrote:*

The wildest thing I have done is to get on my hands and knees and allow my girlfriend to fuck me with a dildo, calling me her slut, her bitch . . . loved it!

A *thirty-two-year-old bisexual man wrote:*

I had one threesome experience with another couple and I got to try some pretty wild things. I got to perform analingus and sucked a cock for the first time. It was very exciting, and I would love to try it again.

A *forty-two-year-old man wrote:*

I phoned my best friend's wife while I was making love to my wife. The friend's wife is a great woman, fun loving and really open sexually. Well, I called her and told her *everything* I was doing in great detail. I would say things like, "I'm pulling her panties to one side and fingering her lips," then, "The tip of my cock is sliding slowly between the smooth lips of her wet pussy," etc. I knew that her husband wasn't home that evening and during the call the lady told me that she was masturbating.

The following afternoon she spoke to my wife as if everything was normal! She did, however, mention that she and her husband had had great sex when he got home.

A fifty-four-year-old man wrote:

My partner and I went to an adult shop that had live dancers. We went into the booth, fed in money, and watched them. After a few minutes, my lady gave me a blow job while the dancers watched us.

A fifty-six-year-old man wrote:

I like to play with my wife's body almost anywhere. While we're shopping I like to caress her when no one is watching.

One time, when we were checking in at a hotel counter, I knew she had on only thong underwear under a relatively short skirt. I stood behind her, fondled her buns, and played with her pussy and asshole while we checked in. No one else was in the lobby of course!

A forty-seven-year-old man wrote:

I guess it was a threesome several years ago. It was really awful because it was sort of by accident. My girlfriend, her friend, and I had dinner and somehow we ended up in bed together. I took turns fucking each of them, and although the friend was not that good in bed, I sort of went nuts at the thought of the situation and came inside her. Then I couldn't get it up to finish my girl. She got super mad, and we later had a fight. It was awful.

A *twenty-five-year-old woman* wrote:

Had it in my boss's office on the conference desk! What a gas!

A *twenty-five-year-old woman* wrote:

Several months ago I took naughty pictures of my fiancé. He'd die if I told even you exactly what they were. Now we look at them and it leads to a night of great sex.

A *thirty-six-year-old woman* wrote:

I had sex with three guys at the same time.

A *fifty-nine-year-old man* wrote:

I like to tie my wife up on the bed. I have some soft rope and I tie her hands in front of her and her legs wide open so I can do whatever I want. Once I put grapes in her pussy, then ate them out one at a time.

TELL ME ABOUT YOUR MOST RECENT SEXUAL EXPERIENCE

Do your neighbors have great sex all the time? I wondered, too, so I asked those responding to the survey to recount their most recent experience. Wishful thinking in a few cases? You be the judge.

A *twenty-one-year-old woman* wrote:

Last night I went over to my boyfriend's house and we started out lying on the couch kissing and then moved into his bedroom where one thing led to another. I performed oral sex on him and made him come, and then I stroked him until he became erect again and he performed anal sex on me. It was a great experience. Very exciting, very satisfying for both of us.

A *forty-seven-year-old man* wrote:

My most recent sex was with my wife in the middle of the night. I was asleep and was sort of nudged awake as she got up to go to the bathroom. She came back to bed several minutes later. As I was falling back to sleep I felt her move and soon she was sucking on my cock. I couldn't pass up an offer like that so I turned her onto her back and we made love for a while. After a bit I flipped her over and I did her doggy-style. She came first, that way, and then I turned her over and came in the missionary position.

A *twenty-six-year-old woman wrote:*

My boyfriend and I live an hour and a half apart so we rarely have much alone time. Our last experience was a quickie for me. Sigh!

A *nineteen-year-old woman wrote:*

The last day my husband had off this month we had the best sex. He ran a bubble bath and surrounded the tub with candles. First we just soaked in the tub for about an hour. Then he set up the bedroom with candles all around. He used cherry-flavored heating massage oil to give me a full-body massage. After about an hour of the massaging, we made love for what seemed like forever. It was wonderful and romantic.

A *forty-eight-year-old man wrote:*

Believe it or not, the last time was in the backseat of a van after shopping.

A *twenty-year-old woman wrote:*

That would have been the sex with my boyfriend when I came back from my Christmas holiday. I was supposed to be going to the library during my lunch hour but he practically dragged me to bed and we had unusually good sex. He then spoiled this great start by telling me to piss off and go to the library. He showed no interest in hugging or talking to me. Grr.

A *twenty-two-year-old man wrote:*

My most recent experience was superb. My partner decided to perform for me for the first time. She is usually inhibited but what got into her this evening I have no idea.

We put on some sexy music—Madonna's *Erotica* album—and she got up on the coffee table. Wearing a skimpy dress, with a see-through underwear set, and knee-high leather boots, she danced for me, sliding her hands all over her body. She removed her dress, and began to gyrate. I couldn't take my eyes off her.

When I thought I was going to shoot in my pants, she removed her bra and began to caress her breasts. She lay down on the table and placed her hand inside her wet panties, masturbating while still moving her body to the music. Finally she removed her undies so that she was wearing only her boots, and stood right in front of my face, still masturbating.

With my eyes on her all the time, she got into the doggy-style position and started to wiggle her ass in front of me. I couldn't take any more by this point so I got up and began to lick her anus. Her body began to spasm and she turned over so I could lick her cunt. Then she stopped me, pushed me back into my seat, and sucked my cock and twisted my nipples. Then she stopped and lay back down on the table, still rubbing herself. She told me to stand over her, and masturbate all over her breasts. As she began to come, so did I, shooting all over her body. I am hoping that she will perform for me again sometime soon, and maybe next time we might use a camera.

A thirty-three-year-old woman wrote:

A few night ago, after reading some of your book *Velvet Whispers,* I was in the mood for some experimenting. After I verified that my boyfriend was okay with it, I took out a vibrating egg that we had bought a few months ago. I had never used this on him and I wanted to know how it would feel. I sat down between his legs and started to run it around his crotch in little circles. As I neared his penis I could see it stretch and grow.

I went over his balls and back to his anus, watching his face to see how much he enjoyed what I was doing and asking if it felt good. He told me it was fantastic and his cock agreed. I couldn't resist the temptation, so I took him in my mouth. With his penis in my mouth and the vibration on his prostate, he just went up the wall.

After a few minutes, since I wanted more than this, I straddled his crotch. I was so wet just seeing him enjoy my ministrations that it was easy to impale myself on him. When I pressed the egg against my clitoris we both went ballistic. He said that he could feel the vibration through my body. Let me tell you that we had reached orgasm at the same time, which never happened before.

A sixty-year-old man wrote:

I have to confess that my most recent sex was not with my wife. I arranged to meet my woman friend from another part of the country, for a day. She came by train and we told her husband and my wife that we were going to visit an exhibition in the trade fair in Amsterdam. In reality we drove to a hotel and had a room from thirteen to seventeen hundred hours. During that time we were in bed constantly and made love in ways neither of us had experienced in our own marriages! We had oral sex and did all kinds of things, both screaming with joy when coming.

A thirty-eight-year-old man wrote:

My wife came to bed late a few nights ago. I was already asleep so she stripped naked and woke me by getting me hard with her hand, then with her mouth.

A thirty-three-year-old woman wrote:

My most recent, ha ha, was five years ago. I am now talking to a guy on the Internet and we are planning on getting together. I'm so much more knowledgeable now and he will most definitely be the best I've ever had.

A thirty-one-year-old man wrote:

My girlfriend came over to my house last evening and I cooked dinner for her. Then we made love in the living room while watching porn and matching what they were doing on the TV.

A forty-seven-year-old woman wrote:

My husband and I work at the same place. The last time we did it we were in the office supply room up against the filing cabinets. Really intense!

I'd love to know more details about that one.

A twenty-three-year-old woman wrote:

My husband and I have just entered the world of light bondage. I say light because we're not really into whips or pain but tying each other up is great. To feel totally powerless with someone who loves you having free rein over you, up to and including having total control of your orgasm, is a powerful drug!!!

A twenty-five-year-old woman wrote:

Last night my boyfriend and I were trying to have sex in a hurry because his friends were coming over. The stress got to him and he kept falling out. Not one of his better moments; in fact that was a first for us.

A twenty-seven-year-old woman wrote:

The other night I wanted him so while we were cuddling on the couch I reached into his shorts and kept fondling him until he was nice and hard. Then I wiggled my bottom against him until he started fondling my nipples.

He tuned the TV to a porno station for a little bit, just to get us a little hornier. I slipped out of my clothes, suggested he do the same, and we just rubbed up against each other for a bit. I pressed against him and whispered, "Please?" He entered me from behind, while one hand was rubbing my clit, and the other was rolling my nipples between his fingers. I pressed my body against him to meet his strokes until he came.

A thirty-year-old woman wrote:

My most recent was with a long-term fling. We call each other when one of us is in the mood—just a sex thing. It's always late at night and is very hot and passionate. Generally we only get an hour or two of sleep. This time, it started out without foreplay but it ended up being a very long session. We slept for a couple of hours and woke up and had sex again.

A *forty-five-year-old woman* wrote:

My most recent experience was with a nondescript lover in a relationship I knew wasn't going to go anywhere. There was no spark, no joie de vivre, no electrical pulses in our lovemaking. He was on top, I was on the bottom, and I didn't have an orgasm. I got, as they say, "fucked."

A *thirty-two-year-old woman* wrote:

It was *fun* and just last night! Anyway, my hubby and I went to a local sex shop and picked up a couple of things: a new whip, a new feather, some ben wa balls, a cock ring, and anal beads. When we got home, he put on his cock ring and I slipped in the ben wa balls. Then we spent the evening enjoying our little secret while we hung out with some friends.

The friends left and we put the kids to bed. We put on an X-rated movie and, when my husband got frisky, I flashed him my pussy and he jumped in!! He pulled my ben wa balls out and gave me head on the living room sofa. After my first orgasm of the night we finished watching the movie! Then we went to the bedroom where he took his time kissing, stroking, licking, and nibbling all over my body. He broke in our new whip and feather on me . . . the switch between the sting of the whip and the tickle of the feather was wonderful! Mmmm. Orgasm number two was quickly followed by orgasm number three when he slipped between my legs and pounded me *hard,* and number four happened when I held him inside me after he had come and rubbed my clit so I could come with him inside me again! As you might have gathered I've recently become multiorgasmic. What a gas!

After that I lost count of how many times I came. Whew!! We grabbed towels to cover the enormous wet spots all over the bed and cuddled up into each other's arms. It was pure heaven!! We never did use the anal beads . . . but there's always tonight!

A thirty-four-year-old woman wrote:

A few nights ago my husband and I weren't planning on sex, we were just going to play a little. It got so hot that we couldn't take it anymore. When my husband slipped inside me I came almost instantly.

A thirty-eight-year-old woman wrote:

My most recent experience happened about two months ago. My husband and I have sex infrequently but when we do it's almost always satisfying. That time I masturbated while he watched, and as I was just about to come, he rammed into me. Since it had been so long since I had had intercourse, I came very fast and very hard. I was very vocal, so vocal that he stopped for fear of waking our teenage children.

A forty-two-year-old woman wrote:

Okay, here goes. My husband is a sweet guy but he has a hard time with an erection and he can't keep it long enough to penetrate. Therefore, sadly, intercourse is out of the question. That last time even the oral sex wasn't all that good because he didn't take his time.

This letter saddens me because Viagra really works!

A forty-seven-year-old woman wrote:

A few nights ago my boyfriend called and wanted to come over but I was in a foul mood so I told him no.

The next day I was off from work and he stopped by early in the morning after my son went to school. I'm afraid that I still didn't feel like it. I guess he really was in the mood so the next thing I know he had me up against the wall, my leg over his shoulder and his tongue going to town. Needless to say, I got in the mood very quickly.

A fifty-eight-year-old woman wrote:

My partner and I live on opposite coasts so we try to get together whenever business or personal travel will allow. Our most recent opportunity was a couple of weeks ago when he came east on business. We took a trip to New Hampshire and Maine to see the foliage.

We made reservations at a wonderful inn in the mountains and arrived fairly late at night. Knowing we would be too tired for dinner, I had packed champagne, wine, cheese, fruit, and crackers in a picnic basket for our first night together. Of course one of the best parts of not being together all the time is that we build up a real hunger for each other. We find it difficult to keep our hands off each other, so the long ride to the mountains was spent playing.

Although we didn't bring each other to orgasm during the drive, preferring to save that for later, we built the anticipation and tension by stimulating each other almost to the point of no return. I'm always sure to wear something with "easy access" and he always wears the silk boxers that I love. I start by rubbing his crotch, opening his fly, and playing with his hard-on before putting my head in his lap and sucking his cock. He loves driving this way, especially if he thinks others know what's going on.

One of the reasons I love his hands is because they know just how to drive me wild. While driving he caresses me, fondling my neck, my breasts, my clit, and finally inserting knowing fingers in my warm, wet channel. It's a delightful way to travel, and when we arrive we are so eager that we make love for hours in every possible position. A wonderful way to enjoy the great outdoors.

If you decide to play this way, please pull your car over. I worry a lot about the accidents that might be caused by "distracted driving."

A *thirty-year-old man wrote:*

Recently I was awakened at two in the morning by my wife's mouth on my cock. The slight confusion of being half asleep made me act raunchy so I just bucked my hips as I came in her mouth paying no attention to her excitement.

A *thirty-one-year-old man wrote:*

Most recently I had unexpected phone sex. A lady friend called me up supposedly just to chat. She'd recently broken up with her boyfriend and was telling me about how much she was enjoying playing the field. We were talking about nothing in particular when she suddenly said, "Oh. I just got off."

"What?"

"I just got myself off just now."

We talked about that a little and continued chatting. Then she said that she had just done it again. Curious about what was going on, I asked her what she was wearing.

"Oh, nothing," she replied.

Well, let me tell you I was really horny by then. The conversation got more and more intimate and eventually she was telling me exactly what she was doing and I was giving her a "blow by blow" of my activities. It was so hot, both because of the dirty talk and because it was so unexpected.

A *thirty-two-year-old man wrote:*

Just a few nights ago my wonderful wife warmed me up with her spectacular fellatio, then asked me if I was ready to try something new. I gave her the okay so she got out a vibrating butt plug and sensuously inserted it in my ass. That sent me to the moon so she climbed on top of me.

Although she was very wet it took a while for me to get inside because she was squeezing so hard (she must think training her Kegel muscles is an Olympic event). After we managed to get my cock inside her she started a slow up-and-down motion.

Somehow the anal stimulation allowed me to last longer so she was able to come three times before I emptied myself into her. It left a terrible wet spot on the bed, but these little inconveniences are well worth it.

A forty-five-year-old man wrote:

During the past couple of weeks circumstances haven't encouraged a really big production number. My most recent experience was nothing more profound than my partner performing oral and manual sex until I ejaculated. It's past time for me to suggest something a bit more. Thanks for getting me to think about it.

A forty-seven-year-old man wrote:

I was spending an evening with a recently divorced former coworker. She had insisted that we'd just be friends and get together for company.

We were sitting on the couch talking and watching TV. Somehow I managed to breathe lightly on her neck. Well, that turned out to be her "hot spot." Woweee!! Right there in front of me she unwound like an overly tightened clock spring and jumped my bones.

A fifty-year-old man wrote:

Unfortunately, my wife and I both work and many nights we're just too tired (how sad is that!). We tend to go on streaks where for a time period we'll do it all the time, maybe three or four times in a week, and then we'll go for a week or longer with nothing. That's the way it's been lately.

Anyway, back to your question. The other night we had a pretty standard lovemaking session for us: half an hour or more of foreplay, kissing and rubbing backs, fronts, etc. and then about fifteen to twenty minutes of actual intercourse. We did it in several different positions—mostly side to side, or her on top. She's been in a sexual slump of late and unfortunately didn't climax. I asked whether there was anything I could do, but she said no and went to sleep.

A fifty-two-year-old man wrote:

My wife and I took a shower together a few night ago, enjoying washing each other's genitals and asses. We spread a thick pile throw on the bedroom floor, gathered our supplies (towels, lube), and turned on our XXX satellite channel for background.

My wife began to suck my cock (which was incredibly hard from the Viagra I had taken). After a nice sucking session, she lay back and I feasted on her smooth, wet pussy for a while, licking and probing. Finally I entered her and, being hot, it didn't take long before we were enjoying full deep strokes. She began rubbing her clit as I thrust into her. Usually we end up orgasming doggy-style, but this time we went totally missionary. It wasn't what you'd call a wham-bam quickie; it was sort of in between, but hot and satisfying for us both.

A fifty-four-year-old man wrote:

I take a blood pressure medication that makes it difficult to get a full erection. It's very frustrating. I get a little hard and come okay but all too often I am not hard enough to penetrate her vagina. I have to think of all sorts of things to get hard enough to insert myself and by then I'm coming just as I enter her.

We have tried playing games, and last year I shaved my pubic hair. It made me crazy with desire, but she hates it. I did it again this year and she wouldn't let me fuck her until it grew out again.

We found that the easiest time to make love is early in the morning. I sleep nude and she sleeps with panties and a T-shirt. Several mornings ago I pulled her close, yanked her panties off, and kissed her vagina. She took off her shirt and started kissing me. She sucked my penis until it was hard enough to penetrate her. She reached for the lube and rubbed it while I stroked her vagina and clitoris gently. Then I entered her. As we moved together and kissed wildly, I thought about how much I really love her and just how lucky I am to have her in my life.

Sex is important and can be rewarding at any age. As this man found out, if there are erectile problems the best time to make love is early in the morning, when his testosterone level is at its highest.

If you're having such problems, please talk to your doctor about your blood pressure medicine. He might be able to prescribe something that doesn't affect your ability to maintain an erection. And talk to him about Viagra. As I said before, it *works!*

A fifty-six-year-old man wrote:

My lady and I don't live in the same state and it's often several months between visits. Since we work in different offices of the same firm, we do get to spend time together at business meetings, as we did last month. As good as the weeks together are, the partings are really tough. Unfortunately, as the week ends, I get depressed about the fact that we won't be together and often I am unable to have an orgasm.

The last time, as we were packing our bags to leave, I made love to her and after I had made her come, although she tried everything, I couldn't. The following morning, on our way to the airport, we parked in a secluded area, where we got in the backseat like teenagers and she gave me the most wonderful blow job! I certainly was able to climax that way.

A twenty-five-year-old woman wrote:

We were at my partner's place, sitting on the sofa watching a movie on his new DVD surround-sound system. He has amazing hands and started to caress me through my clothing. He knows exactly where to touch, without me having to tell him.

Anyhow, we were kissing and petting when he just picked me up. Giggling, I wrapped my legs around him while he walked us to the bedroom. Once there we removed all our clothes. I lay on top of his gorgeous body and began lightly rubbing my wetness along his hard penis. Then he was inside me, thrusting deeper and deeper. I stopped him and told him that it would be a good idea to put on a condom so that he wouldn't have to keep stopping when he thought he would come. With a condom in place he continued where he left off, slowly inserting his penis in me and vigorously thrusting harder and faster. It felt amazing. I wrapped my legs around his waist, ran my hands down toward his butt, and pulled him closer.

To his disappointment he came quickly so he began to lick and suck my pussy madly while his fingers thrust inside. Within minutes I came, but he continued to suck and finger me. He rubbed an area inside me that made my whole body quiver. He thinks he may have found my g-spot, but I was so deep into the pleasure that all I knew was that I didn't want him to stop. We are planning on exploring that area more in the future.

Beware! Those first few drops of pre-come that lubricate a man's penis are filled with sperm and can contain disease organisms. If you're using a condom for birth or disease control, put that condom on before *any* contact between penis and vagina.

A *twenty-five-year-old woman wrote:*

For us it was average. The baby finally went to sleep and we jumped into bed. We masturbated together then I sucked him for a few minutes. Then he went down on me (my favorite part). Then we made love for about two and a half hours. That's about an average length of time for us.

A *thirty-year-old woman wrote:*

My most recent was just your plain "let's do it and get it over with."

A *fifty-one-year-old man wrote:*

I am "gimped up" with Parkinson's disease. My penis still gets hard, but I cannot move very well. I still love sex, though, and so does my wife.

Most recently she took off her flannel nightshirt, reached down, and started stroking me. I got hard right away. She took the upper position, inserting my penis, then moving up and down, putting her breasts in my face. I asked her to slow down, to prolong it, because it felt so good to me. It was such great physical relief when I came. I told her that it felt like "heaven on earth."

A sixty-two-year-old man wrote:

Two nights ago our kids and grandkids had finally gone home after a long Christmas visit. My wife and I had had a bit of quiet subdued sex while they were visiting but this was the first good sex in two weeks. I gave her a back rub, we cuddled, worked up to a rowdy sixty-nine, then finished with our favorite doggy-style. Warm, wonderful, and terrifically noisy!

WHAT DO YOU WISH YOUR PARTNER KNEW? WHAT DO YOU WISH HE OR SHE WOULD TELL YOU?

This section combines two questions. The first was: What do you wish your partner would tell you about making love? Many men and women said that they wished their partner would tell them exactly what the partner wanted or exactly what he or she was feeling. Amen. Good communication is the key to making lovemaking the best it can be.

A *nineteen-year-old woman* wrote:

> I wish he would tell me how he likes to receive oral sex. By this I mean, what feels good and what doesn't. Sometimes I wonder if what I'm doing is pleasurable or not.

A *twenty-year-old woman* wrote:

> I'd like him to give me more directions. I do my best, but he isn't very good at telling me what feels good.

Have you ever asked? Yes, I do mean asked. Have you ever said, "Does this feel good?" Of course your partner will say yes, but you can probably tell how strong that yes is. A better question might be, "What can I do to make it better?" If your partner says,

"Nothing," just say, "Please help me. I really want to know."

I'm sure you can understand that your partner probably feels the same way. I know it's risky and embarrassing to say, "Do it this way," but there are other methods of communication. You can give your partner help, even if you can't say the words. Moan, purr, give your partner a clue that what he or she is doing feels good. Grab hair and guide your partner; use your hands to demonstrate. It's really much easier than you might think, and your partner will be grateful.

A twenty-six-year-old woman wrote:

> I wish he would tell me some of his fantasies. I would love to hear about them and maybe make some of them come true.

A fifty-nine-year-old man wrote:

> I'd like to know her sexual fantasies. I have asked and she says that she does not have any. I think she does and sharing them would be fun and might lead to some great things.

A forty-seven-year-old man wrote:

> I just wish she would say yes more often.

A thirty-two-year-old man wrote:

> I think she's told me everything she knows, but I think she needs to know more about herself. Maybe some talking would help both of us understand.

A thirty-six-year-old woman wrote:

> I wish he knew that, because I believe that I'm not attractive, his saying how much he wants me would really help put me in the mood.

A sixty-year-old man wrote:

> I want to know exactly what turns her on most, how and when she experiences orgasm(s), and . . . whether she would like anal sex.

A thirty-three-year-old woman wrote:

I wish he would tell me that he loves me. Often.

A thirty-one-year-old man wrote:

I wish she would say whether there is anything else she wants me to do to make her happy.

A fifty-one-year-old woman wrote:

What do I want to hear? Easy. That I'm the best he's ever had.

A thirty-one-year-old man wrote:

I wish she would tell me why she limits our intercourse to once a month, and what I can do to encourage her to express herself sexually.

I also asked the other side of the question: "What do you wish your partner knew about making love with you?" Here are a few of the answers.

A fifty-one-year-old woman wrote:

There is nothing he doesn't know about me. From the start of our relationship he's always wanted to know what felt best and I've always told him. It felt a bit daunting at first, but now it's just part of our lovemaking.

A forty-seven-year-old woman wrote:

I wish my husband really knew how much I love his lovemaking and how special and beautiful he makes me feel. All I have to do is look at him and I have an orgasmic experience!!!!!

Several people want their partner's attitude to be a bit different.

A fifty-four-year-old man wrote:

I wish she would be more adventurous.

A fifty-nine-year-old man wrote:

I wish she would be a little more assertive. Most of the time it's fine with me giving the directions and her following, but sometimes I wish she would be more liberated.

A twenty-six-year-old woman wrote:

I wish he knew that I like creativity. Not necessarily bondage and fetish stuff, but just doing something I hadn't expected—twisting into a new position or trying something different.

Others had specific things. I just wonder why the writer hasn't told his or her partner. It's not as difficult as it might seem. Asking for something different can be done in a way that doesn't hurt anyone's feelings. "I love it when you . . . I wish you would do it more." "You feel so good, but a lighter touch would feel even better."

A sixty-eight-year-old man wrote:

I wish she knew better how to suck cock.

A thirty-three-year-old woman wrote:

I wish he understood that he has to give me a minute after I climax because my clit is very sensitive.

A nineteen-year-old woman wrote:

I wish he knew that I don't like my clit to be rubbed a lot. He thinks he's driving me wild but sometimes it gets irritating. Another thing is that, since I had our daughter, I am very tender down there where they did the episiotomy. He isn't very gentle sometimes and it can really hurt.

A twenty-year-old woman wrote:

I wish he knew that I need more foreplay! Lots more foreplay! I always announce that I'm coming. So if I have not said it, then I haven't come and he might want to do something about it. Since

I went on the pill and we stopped using condoms he has been very bad about helping me come.

And lastly, I wish he knew that sometimes I need to be hugged a bit more afterward. Otherwise I just feel like a receptacle.

A thirty-one-year-old man wrote:

That often a fifteen-minute petting session is more satisfying than a five-minute quickie. I know that's supposed to be a woman's plea but it's just as true for me.

A thirty-six-year-old woman wrote:

I wish my husband would talk more during lovemaking, like, "Do that again," or, "Touch here." He says everything I do is great. Maybe he is afraid that he'll sound like he's barking orders at me but I really want to know.

A twenty-one-year-old woman wrote:

It's pretty simple. The faster and harder, the better.

A sixty-year-old man wrote:

I wish she understood that oral sex with her does turn me on and how much I enjoy tasting her vulva and just eating her for hours.

IS THERE A SEXUAL THING YOU ONCE DID THAT YOU NOW REGRET?

Many people lamented their missed opportunities. Maybe that says something to us! In addition, many wrote that they now regret they had sex with a person they didn't care about: one-night stands and the like. I had a lot of one-night stands in the dating years after my divorce and, though many were less than fabulous, I don't regret any of them. They were all learning experiences. I explored my feelings about myself, my likes, my dislikes, most important, I learned a lot about my sexuality.

Okay, so what do I regret? I'm sure there were many times that, in my younger days with a monumental ignorance of sexual matters, I insulted or otherwise hurt the feelings of a partner. Although I don't remember specifics, I'm sure I squashed someone's ego or made light of something my partner took seriously. Unfortunately, it's easy to do, and I regret that immensely.

What did others regret?

A *thirty-three-year-old woman* wrote:

I really regret my first time. It was the wrong person and, unfortunately, I became pregnant. I don't regret my child—she's a wonderful little girl—but I do regret that I didn't love the man.

A twenty-two-year-old woman wrote:

I regret that I've had casual sex. It hasn't happened often but I have, occasionally, had sex with a man I wasn't attracted to. Now I'm sorry because I usually choose not to be with guys outside relationships.

A twenty-three-year-old woman wrote:

I guess I regret sleeping with most of the partners I did it with. As I look back I realize that, if I had it to do all over, I wouldn't have slept with any of them.

A twenty-five-year-old woman wrote:

Yes! Cheating. No matter what was going on with us at the time, I should have been faithful. Even though there were clear signs that he was cheating, too, I should not have done what I did.

A twenty-seven-year-old man wrote:

I deeply regret cheating on my partner. I regret it because it hurt the girl I had sex with to know I was already spoken for. She really liked me and I was just fucking her. I also hate myself for violating the most important thing in my life—my marriage. Although it's long in the past, I still regret that more than anything.

And this forty-year-old married man doesn't say specifically what he regrets, but it's pretty obvious from what he wrote:

Straying is very bad business. The other person either ends up feeling angry that she ever got involved with you, or she falls in love with you. If love happens, she then wants you to leave your wife for her, then ends up being brokenhearted and angry when you don't. I think it's fine to look and admire another, but mated people need to be just that.

A sixty-eight-year-old man wrote:

I really regret something I did lots of years ago. I seduced an eighteen-year-old virgin when I was in college. I wrote her erotic poems, and eventually her parents found them. I guess it was her fault for keeping them where they could be discovered, but I regret that I created a bad experience for her.

A *thirty-six-year-old woman* wrote:

Yes, there are things I wish I hadn't done. When I was young, I participated in sexual acts out of a need to feel desired. I guess it was my low self-esteem, rather than enjoyment. I think that, in the long run, it lowered my self-esteem further.

A *nineteen-year-old woman* wrote:

The only sexual thing I regret is having been with so many people. I was safe about it every time, but I just wish there hadn't been so many. I know there are women out there who have been with more and my number isn't all that high especially considering how long I've been doing it, but I still have regrets.

A *thirty-three-year-old woman* wrote:

I regret being with my first sexual partner for several reasons. First, I didn't really like him. I wanted to make love with my ex-fiancé and I didn't want to go to him as a virgin so I let another guy, one I didn't even particularly like, "initiate" me. I regret it because my ex-fiancé said that coming to him a virgin would have been the best gift I could have ever given him.

A *fifty-one-year-old woman* wrote:

I remember having sex with a stranger. It was many years ago, before the threat of AIDS and herpes. I danced with a fellow in a club and without any words spoken, left with him to go to his place.

We got undressed and lay down on his bed. He put his cock into me, moved his hips a few times, and then came. Perhaps five minutes later he announced that he didn't like sluts to sleep at his place, so he called me a cab. He made me feel so cheap. All that I was to him was a hole for him to put his cock in.

A thirty-one-year-old man wrote:

I regret taking one of my girlfriends anally even though she ex-
pressed a great interest in it. It was entirely too painful for her
and I still feel very guilty for continuing even though she told me
that it would be okay.

A forty-three-year-old woman wrote:

Many years ago I allowed my then-boyfriend to take my picture
while I sucked his cock. He was a real pervert and kept pictures
of all his conquests. He still has it and I'm afraid it will end up in
my husband's hands someday.

A forty-five-year-old married man wrote:

I regret flirting with an old girlfriend whom I hadn't seen in several years. We had lunch together and played and teased
through the meal. It was stupid to even contemplate anything,
and thankfully, nothing happened. I was tempted, however.

A forty-seven-year-old woman wrote:

I'm really sorry that I once participated in an orgy. It was just sex,
and devoid of anything like fun. I felt lots of pressure to perform
well and I was so nervous that I hated it.

A thirty-nine-year-old woman wrote:

I was molested by a male family member (a cousin) when I was
small. It was all oral, no anal or vaginal stuff. What I regret is that
it stole an innocence that wasn't his to take.

And on the same topic, a fifty-four-year-old woman wrote:

I was molested by my grandfather. Although there was no actual
intercourse, he touched me in the special forbidden places. I
guess I let him do it because, since my mom and dad divorced
when I was small, I was starved for male attention. Now I feel
that it was my fault for letting it happen and not saying no.

To feel guilty for something over which you had no control is so sad. I hope at least one of the women who wrote these answers is reading this now and will talk to a professional. Remember, *you* were the child and *he* was the grown-up. The responsibility is all his!

A fifty-eight-year-old woman wrote:

My best girlfriend and I live in far distant states, and when we visit each other we always spend our first night together "solving the problems of the world" and usually drinking too much. On this visit to her house we were wondering why it's every guy's fantasy to have two women at the same time.

You probably already know how this one goes. We kept drinking, and talking about how her husband (my oldest friend!), who was happily asleep in the bedroom, was always teasing about having both of us in bed at the same time. Well, as the hour and liquor wore on, we decided to give it a go (bad decision!). We staggered down the hall, crawled into their overstuffed king-size bed, and began to arouse him. We didn't actually "do it" but it did go too far.

When I came to my senses, I fled their bedroom for the guest room, wondering whether I could get an early flight home instead of ever seeing them again. Thanks to my friends' understanding and good sense, we talked about it in the morning, placing no blame, and we all decided that it would never happen again. We also prayed no permanent harm had been done to our relationship.

Well, although it caused a temporary rift in our friendship, we've all recovered and our friendship is even stronger now. I'm still haunted, however, by the fact that it could have permanently damaged a relationship that is one of the most important in my life.

A thirty-one-year-old man wrote:

I deeply regret the time that I tried to bargain sex from an exgirlfriend because I knew she still loved me and I was horny. In the end she asked me whether I still loved her. I couldn't even lie to her, and she was very hurt. Sometimes men behave badly.

A forty-one-year-old man wrote:

As a young man I did some homosexual playing around with another boy my age. Those days only pop into my head occasionally but when they do it scares me to death.

A forty-two-year-old man wrote:

While I was dating a fun-loving lady, I took several nude Polaroid photos of her. We didn't really split up, we just sort of mutually decided we weren't going anywhere in our relationship, so she started dating other guys and I kind of entered a dry spell. She let me keep the photos when we went our separate ways. When I later got married, I destroyed them but I wish I had kept them. I would just like to look at them now. I always wondered what became of her.

A forty-five-year-old man wrote:

I think I may have picked up a mild urinary tract or prostate infection when I had unprotected anal intercourse with a woman I was dating several years ago. I went to my doctor and, on his advice, I took a full course of antibiotics. The infection seems to have been cured.

I just want you to know that I didn't regret the sex, which was superb, but the urinary frequency was no fun. Now I plan ahead. Always.

A forty-eight-year-old man wrote:

Once when I was feeling really horny I pressured my wife for anal penetration while she had her period. I really wanted to have plain old sex with her, but she used to get bad cramps if we did.

We used to joke and tease about having anal sex but to that point we hadn't done it. Well, I was so horny I didn't realize that she was telling me to slow down and went ahead and penetrated her. I hurt her, and she resented it a lot, as she should have. I regret having hurt her and, secretly, I regret having poisoned her on anal sex. I would like to try it again, but I know she wouldn't want it. After that, alas, we never did it again.

A fifty-year-old man wrote:

Fifteen years ago, while traveling for work, I got a blow job from a hooker. A male friend and I were away together and we'd both had some drinks. My friend suggested we "rent" a woman who was working the lounge we were in. I was curious, so I succumbed and I regret it to this day. I felt as if I let my wife, and worst of all myself, down.

A fifty-six-year-old man wrote:

A couple of years ago I met a lady for sex whom I had previously only known through the Internet. She was not what I imagined she would be, and I probably hurt her feelings.

A seventy-four-year-old man wrote:

My biggest regret is the night I had sex for the first time with my high school steady, no protection, no nothing. It seemed great at the time but, as I look back on it, we were too young and reckless. Our whole lives could have been changed. It's really scary.

A thirty-year-old woman wrote:

I regret having sex with a boyfriend and then giving a blow job to his older brother while he watched. He said it was a fantasy, but why with his brother? You're the only person I've ever told.

A thirty-eight-year-old woman wrote:

I regret having had anal sex with my ex-husband. I regret it because I gave that part of myself to him when he never really loved me. And most of the time it hurt and he never cared. He was so selfish.

A sixty-two-year-old man wrote:

In the late 1960s, early 1970s, I did a lot of swinging. It was fun and I enjoyed it; my wife at the time did, too, at first. Eventually, however, she grew disillusioned but I was addicted and all but insisted that we continue.

Now I know that she endured to please me, but in the end it broke us up. It was a bittersweet experience for me. I still have some good sex memories but I know I hurt her and am not proud of it. *Young and stupid* sums it up. The idea still appeals to me, but both partners must be equally committed.

four

ORAL AND ANAL SEX

DO YOU AND YOUR PARTNER ENGAGE IN ORAL SEX?

The statistics were almost exactly the same for men and women: 96% of the men and 95% of the women who responded said that they engage in oral sex.

Most of the answers, across all age groups and both sexes, were short and sweet and decidedly positive.

A sixty-eight-year-old man wrote:

Oh yes!! I love it. I worship clits and vulvas, and love the smell, taste, and texture.

A twenty-one-year-old woman wrote:

Oral sex is *great* foreplay! I honestly enjoy giving more than receiving but I cannot complain there either! I love knowing that I am pleasuring him while it is a major turn-on for me as well.

A thirty-one-year-old man wrote:

I can't get enough of her taste. She is cleanly shaven, so I would go down on her for hours if she'd let me.

A fifty-one-year-old woman wrote:

I enjoy it very much. I love the feeling of a rock-hard cock in my mouth, and it's great knowing that I'm driving him to the brink time and again before I let him come deep in my throat.

A forty-seven-year-old woman wrote:

I love it when he performs oral sex on me, and he has told me that he loves to watch me perform oral sex on him, because, he says, I really enjoy it and my facial expressions show it.

A seventy-eight-year-old man wrote:

I love it both ways. It's soooooooo intimate.

A twenty-seven-year-old woman wrote:

I enjoy doing it a lot. I feel a lot of power doing that to him, controlling how much pleasure he'll receive and when. He doesn't give me oral sex, though. Occasionally I've told him that if I do it for him he should do it for me. Fair is fair.

For this couple oral sex had become a bargaining chip. I'll do for you if you'll . . . In my opinion, that's not what it's all about. View oral sex as two different activities. If you enjoy fellatio (where she performs on him) and/or cunnilingus (where he performs on her), then great. Do what feels good and not what doesn't. Don't make it a "tit for tat" arrangement.

Quite a few respondents wrote that the male partner enjoys giving while the female doesn't enjoy it as much.

A forty-seven-year-old man wrote:

Yes, we do have oral sex occasionally. She goes hot and cold about it. When she is in the mood to give oral to me it is absolutely fantastic. I love giving oral to her anytime.

A twenty-two-year-old man wrote:

I love to give oral sex, but she does not. She does it occasionally, but stops when the pre-come starts because, she says, she doesn't like the taste. She has done it with me wearing a condom but even then she stops after a while. I have not yet come from oral sex. It's a big ambition of mine and my girlfriend has promised to let me cash in at some point.

A *thirty-two-year-old man* wrote:

I enjoy giving her oral sex and I know she enjoys getting it. However, she doesn't like to perform it on me and, of course, I won't insist. I'd love it if she did but she can't bring herself to do it. Oh well, nobody's perfect.

A *fifty-four-year-old woman* wrote:

I don't like oral sex, just can't get used to the taste.

Let me answer the question you men are probably asking: *How can I entice my lady to perform oral sex?* Notice I use the word *entice*, not *force* or *get her to*.

There are several issues involved here, some so deeply psychological that I wouldn't dream of attempting to deal with them. For many women, oral sex is a taboo. Many people's religious beliefs teach them that activities that don't result in conception are forbidden. It's dirty, girls are told, and you'll go to hell if you do it.

When I was in my teens I had been told by my close girlfriends that oral sex was disgusting. Maybe some of them secretly enjoyed it, but they certainly wouldn't have admitted it, not in the late 1950s. In those years, sex before at least engagement was much less common (or maybe just less talked about). So from early on in my dating career, oral sex was a no-no. Nice guys didn't ask for it and nice girls didn't do it. Period.

Guys tried, of course, and that left nasty memories. I remember being in the front seat of a car and having a date insist. It began with a request, then a bargaining chip, then I was all but forced to attempt it. I remember the guy was already hot and sweaty and the smell of him in the hot car was overwhelming. When I bent over to attempt it, he pressed his hand on the back of my head and held me down. I bolted and asked him to take me home, which he did. That, both literally and figuratively, left an almost permanent bad taste in my mouth. I didn't perform oral sex on a lover until I was over forty, and, although I enjoy it when Ed does it for me, giving still isn't my favorite activity.

The first time I performed oral sex on a man was in the bathtub, and that's a strong recommendation. If you want to entice your lady, try doing it in the shower, tub, or pool. That way the natural odors are at a minimum. Lots of soapy foreplay and a little guidance and you might make it.

I know that guys seem to love the smell and taste but that's a bit embarrassing for me, too. I seldom feel like I'm "kissing sweet," as the commercials say, so playing in the bath or shower might allow her to relax and let the guy enjoy himself, too.

There are other issues as well.

A *thirty-five-year-old woman wrote*:

I love what he does for me, but I'm not comfortable doing him. I don't feel that I'm doing it right.

A *sixty-six-year-old man wrote*:

She doesn't do it well and doesn't like it.

Another problem with oral sex, at least for me, is that I want to "do it right." Like me, many women feel that there's some master technique for giving a man oral pleasure—one that we never learned. Therefore, we don't "give good head" and therefore, we'll be a sexual failure when the man finds out. Yes, guys, we actually believe that. So please, help us. Moan a lot. Tell us that it feels fantastic. Gently and in a positive way, suggest things that might make it better. "Darling, I love it just like that." Or, "Umm, do it really slowly"—or "quickly," or whatever. Give lots of positive feedback. No one was born knowing. Be a teacher. Help her learn exactly what you like. If you do that your student can become the best at fellatio, at least for you.

Ladies, there's no "right way," no secret technique that you need to learn. Just relax and do what you think might feel nice for him. You don't have to be Linda Lovelace and deep-throat your guy. Kiss his penis. Lick him like a lollipop. Circle the head of his penis with your tongue. Play with your hands as well as your mouth. If he's not helping with moans and hip gyrations, ask him often whether it feels good. Tease with, "Which feels better, this or that?" Then do two different things. Play with the possibilities.

A *twenty-five-year-old woman* wrote:

I enjoy the receiving end but the giving . . . Well, he always wants me to swallow and I don't like the taste. It makes me gag. Plus after a while, my jaw begins to hurt and I can hardly move it.

A *thirty-eight-year-old woman* wrote:

Yes, it's definitely part of the package, both giving and receiving. However, I do not swallow.

Guys, go easy on requests for swallowing. I'm not sure what the lure of that is, but many women just don't want to, myself included. So, in order to have your lady relax, tell her you'll give her plenty of warning. Then remove your penis from her mouth and never, never surprise her. If you do, she'll be reluctant to ever do it again. If, after you two have been playing for a while, you want to ask whether she'll allow you to come in her mouth, fine. Then abide by her answer.

A *seventy-seven-year-old man* wrote:

I really enjoy oral sex with my partner. I love how she tastes and how her mouth feels on me. We do not "sixty-nine," however. I find it distracting when I'm trying to please her.

Sixty-nine, performing mutual oral sex on each other, doesn't work for me either. I like my pleasures one at a time, so if I'm both performing and receiving, one or the other doesn't get my full attention. Maybe it's like that for you, so you might want to try one thing at a time for starters.

One last thing for both of you. Don't overlook good old chocolate sauce, whipped cream, or really sticky maple syrup. It sounds silly and messy, but it works. And silly is fabulous when approaching something a bit difficult.

With all that in mind, let's see what other folks have to say.

A forty-five-year-old woman wrote:

I absolutely love eating my partner to orgasm. I love playing with my mouth on his penis, engaging it in many ways, tickling it, sucking it, flicking or circling it with my tongue, filling my mouth with wine and swirling it around his cock. I love the power of sucking him to orgasm and then taking it all down my throat. I have learned that many women won't do this for their men, and I can't imagine why not.

A twenty-six-year-old woman wrote:

We haven't yet. When we were first married we were young and inexperienced and both thought oral sex was "yucky." We discussed it and agreed not to do it because we were both uncomfortable with the idea. Now my feelings have changed. I am curious as to how it feels to give and to receive. I haven't reopened the issue with my husband yet because I'm afraid of what he will say.

Don't be afraid. Mention it to him. If he's not interested, you've lost nothing. If he is, then you've opened the door to something you might both enjoy. Go for it!

A fifty-eight-year-old woman wrote:

I'm very oral and I love having his cock in my mouth, knowing that it drives him wild. I don't always like to "complete" the act, preferring to have him inside me when he comes, but sometimes it's really exciting to feel his warm come shoot into my mouth and down my throat.

A thirty-year-old man wrote:

I like to lick her cunt while she is on the phone with friends. The little moans she cannot suppress are worth it.

A thirty-two-year-old man wrote:

My wife and I enjoy oral sex all the time. My favorite thing in the world is to lick and suck her nice juicy pussy through four or five orgasms, while trying to hold on as she thrashes about wildly on the bed. The feel, look, taste, and smell of a woman's sex is intoxicating to me. I love to slide my tongue in between the folds of her labia and savor the flavor of her arousal as I flick and caress her clit with my tongue, alternating between slow and fast movements, bringing her to the edge and then slowing down until she can't take it anymore. Then I suck her whole pussy in my mouth and rapidly flick her clit with my tongue as I apply suction until she explodes.

My wife is an absolute master in the art of fellatio, which is definitely a plus for me. She takes great pride and care in her work as she sucks my cock. She slowly slides up and down and uses her tongue all over. She alternates between light and hard suction, and fast and slow strokes, making me writhe while she lightly fondles my balls. I wish she would swallow, but you can't have everything.

A fifty-one-year-old man wrote:

I enjoy bringing my wife to orgasm with my tongue. I have to laugh because her body shakes violently and she cries out really loudly. I enjoy her kissing my penis but I then like her to move on top and straddle me so I can come deep within her rather than in her mouth and throat. I say this even though she is very good at "deep throat."

A forty-eight-year-old man wrote:

I love to do oral on her, but she won't consider doing it on me. I have trouble just getting her to touch my penis, or balls.

If I really take my time and manage to do it just right, I can make her come from oral, but usually if we do this, I just do it for a while, and then we switch to missionary sex with me fingering her clitty.

A fifty-year-old man wrote:

My wife performs on me pretty regularly, either as foreplay or just for a good time (no coming in her mouth, though). I perform it on her when she'll let me. When I go down on her she loves it and will come if I stay there but she usually stops me and wants to finish au naturel.

A fifty-six-year-old man wrote:

Oral sex was probably one of my favorite sexual fantasies prior to meeting my current lady. She has taken our sexual relationship to such a higher plane in so many areas that although I still enjoy oral sex it is only one of many wonderful ways for us to enjoy each other!

A sixty-eight-year-old man wrote:

I remember the first time my wife and I had oral sex. I kissed her tits, and down across her navel, but she stopped me when she became aware of my apparent destination. I told her I wanted to kiss her "down there" and she asked me why. I told her I just wanted to see what it was like. She agreed but stipulated that no way was she taking me into her mouth. I said, "Fair enough," and moved into the sixty-nine position.

Well, she liked what I did for her so much that a few seconds later, to my surprise and delight, I felt her slide her tongue around my cock. She said afterward that, contrary to her previous thoughts, when she felt the silky head of my cock in her mouth, it was the nicest thing imaginable.

On only a few occasions thereafter we have performed oral on each other, but never to orgasm for either of us. I offered to bring her to climax on a couple of occasions, but she said that it would mean I would get soaked in her juices and that grossed her out.

Here are two great letters. These two folks tell, in their own words, about their first time with oral sex.

A *twenty-four-year-old man wrote:*

I must write about the first time I gave oral sex to a woman. I was twenty and I went to a wedding with a date who was twenty-two. After the wedding we went to her apartment and things got heated with a lot of kissing and fondling. I unzipped her dress and freed her breasts, then began sucking on her nipples.

She got up, put her hand out, and led me upstairs to her bedroom. She then undressed and got into bed as I stood there watching. I quickly took my clothes off and joined her. After a lot of kissing and feeling her breasts, I reached down and felt her slippery wet vagina. I could smell a little odor coming from under the sheets, and this turned me on knowing it was coming from her genitals.

Although I didn't really know what I was doing, I slid down under the covers and began licking her entire crotch area, putting my tongue inside her vagina and running it up to her clitoris. I could reach up and play with her nipples as I licked her vulva. Her vagina tasted a little salty, and it smelled very different from anything I had ever experienced. I think it was the forbidden-area smell that turned me on. I kept licking as she whispered how good it felt. I felt her nipples get real hard sticking up like miniature erections, and her body stiffened up. She was breathing really hard, and whispered that she was going to come.

I will never forget this. It was the first time I brought a woman to orgasm, and the way her body shook and the way she moaned made me more excited. After she came, she rolled a condom on my stiff penis, and then I inserted it into her very wet vagina. After only twenty seconds of in-and-out stuff I came in an explosive manner.

A twenty-three-year-old woman wrote:

The first time I gave oral sex to a man was a memorable time for me. It was also the first time for my boyfriend.

It was a very hot summer afternoon and we were both wearing shorts and T-shirts. While sitting on the couch and watching the *Ricki Lake* show my boyfriend and I began kissing. As I had done before, I put my hand up his pant leg, and the feel of his hard penis really turned me on. I pulled his shorts off and he pulled his T-shirt off over his head. As he sat there naked I played with his stiff penis and rubbed his testicles as I tried to get the courage to put my mouth on his erection.

We got into a pattern where I was stimulating his genitals slowly as we still watched the TV. I noticed that after a while when I pulled down on the shaft of his penis some clear fluid seeped out. For some reason I wanted to taste it so I licked him. Well, my boyfriend moaned really loud when my lips touched the head of his penis.

I remember how warm his erection felt on my lips, and how soft the skin was. Then I licked and kissed around the head while holding it by the shaft. His excitement level rose as I licked away. I then took the head of the penis into my mouth and began rubbing my tongue around it. As I stroked and sucked it I could feel his body tense up in pleasure.

I wasn't ready to have him shoot in my mouth so, when I could feel him ready to ejaculate, I licked under the head while stroking the shaft. As I watched, semen came blasting out. We were both delighted, for different reasons.

DO YOU AND YOUR PARTNER ENGAGE IN ANAL SEX?

A *thirty-three-year-old woman* wrote:

> I don't enjoy anal sex and neither does my husband, but when he touches my anus during sex it really turns me on.

Anal sex and anal intercourse are two different things. Anal sex—touching, stroking, or licking the area around the anus—might end up with anal penetration and anal intercourse, but it doesn't have to. There are many people of both sexes who enjoy (or might enjoy) having their anal area touched during lovemaking who wouldn't enjoy penetration of any sort. Others might enjoy a slender toy or finger inserted but are worried that something as large as a penis would cause pain. If you want to experiment, go for it, even if it never leads to penetration. Just a touch can heighten arousal for lots of people.

Many of the folks who responded to my survey had never tried anal sex and had no interest in it. That's fine. My motto is, If It Feels Good, Do It. The corollary is, If It Doesn't, Don't!

A *forty-six-year-old man* wrote:

> No . . . my wife doesn't like it.

A *seventy-seven-year-old man* wrote:

No, we don't practice anal sex, even though I would like to. On several occasions when I've been performing oral sex on her, I've touched her anus and felt her draw back. It's really not that big a deal to me so I don't push her. Why spoil a good thing?

Bravo!

Others surveyed said that they want to try but are afraid. If you want to play, here are a few guidelines. First, lots of foreplay. It relaxes the muscles as well as the inhibitions. Then use lots of lubricant—lots and lots of water-based lubricant! Try K-Y Jelly or the one I like, Astroglide. No oil-based lubes like baby oil. They can eat through condoms and make tiny holes that can let disease organisms through.

Make everything very slippery. Play with touches, toys, what-have-you, and discover whether it's pleasurable. If a touch is exciting and you want to go farther, great. If not, you've still discovered something enjoyable.

If you want to try penetration, always use a condom and remove it immediately after withdrawal. Avoid any contact with the vaginal area after you've played anally, whether with a finger, toy, or condom-covered penis. Even the slightest touch can transfer really nasty bacteria from the anus to the vagina, causing a serious infection.

One final and most important word—anal penetration of any kind is a *high-risk activity!* Several life-threatening diseases—AIDS, hepatitis, and more—are transmitted through blood-to-blood contact. During anal sex there is often a tiny amount of blood released—often not even enough to see, but enough to contain a lethal number of viruses. Always use one (or even two) condoms and be really careful. *Really careful.*

A *thirty-six-year-old woman* wrote:

My hubby and I really enjoy anal sex, but we have some rules. I am the boss and we have it only when I say I am ready. When I say "wait" or "hold it" it means stop and don't move in or out. Once my sphincter muscles relax we then continue.

A twenty-one-year-old woman wrote:

I have only done it a couple of times and for now I don't think I'd do it on a regular basis. It is more painful than anything else that I have experienced sexually. I still enjoy it because he does, but I give in only when I want to.

A thirty-six-year-old man wrote:

We have never tried putting my cock into her that way, but we do play with fingers. I would love to fuck her ass but she can barely take my cock in her pussy—she is small. I'm afraid that anal sex would injure her.

A forty-five-year-old woman's response leads me to an important point. She wrote:

Anal sex doesn't turn me on at all. Fortunately, no partner has ever pressured me into having anal sex.

I react very strongly to her word *pressured*. Never, never do something because a partner pressures you to do it. Whatever the activity, do things because you want to, or because you're curious, or even because it will give you a tremendous amount of pleasure to do something he really will enjoy. But make sure that if you say "stop," he will. Period.

A sixty-eight-year-old bisexual man, now married to a woman, has two different takes on anal sex. He wrote:

I've never done it with my wife because she is afraid of it. I have fucked only one woman in the ass. In my opinion, with women it's just a diversion.

My gay friends ask for it so I do it with them, or rather I try. I have difficulty staying hard with male partners, probably because of the condoms that are so essential. Usually I get in deep as he lies on his back and then I stroke his cock until he comes. After that it usually takes only a few strokes for me to come as well.

A forty-seven-year-old man wrote:

We have had anal sex three times. It hurt her. I really wanted to play and not to have it hurt, but we never were able to get a handle on it.

A forty-eight-year-old man wrote:

I enjoy it a lot but I think she only does it for me. The last time (this is embarrassing) I was kidding her about giving me her ass in exchange for a new living room set. She agreed (after a lot of convincing), and I tried everything to make it good. Still, it hurt her a bunch and I stopped midstream, only about three inches into her butt. A few weeks later she bought her new living room set.

A thirty-six-year-old woman wrote:

If you mean him putting his penis in my ass, no. No! But when we're in the right mood, we use toys in the anal area and that's a kick. We've got a really slender dildo with a vibrator inside. It's skinny and flexible enough to bend where it needs to. Once I'm really hot, he uses lots of lube and slides it in. If I don't come right then, he turns on the little motor and I go off like a rocket. Sometime I'd like to use it on him. I think he'd really like it. Maybe soon!

A twenty-year-old woman wrote:

I would be interested in trying actual anal sex, but my boyfriend is only just becoming comfortable with anal play. He used to think it was incredibly icky, but since I'd like to try it, he has come around to the idea. Now he touches me and it really lights me up.

Let me admit right now that I can, and do, push things inside my bottom with ease when masturbating, but only at the right angle and after some stroking and clitoral stimulation. His penis is way bigger than my mascara, and he's a darn sight less gentle with it. Maybe, someday.

A fifty-one-year-old woman wrote:

I love it. At first I did it to please him, although I really thought it was dirty, but when we tried it I had to admit to him how incredible it felt. My moans gave me away.

A twenty-five-year-old woman wrote:

I really don't like it much, but I do it to please my partner. Since he gets so much joy out of it, I'm willing, and I find his pleasure becomes my pleasure.

A twenty-six-year-old woman wrote:

It hurts but I have been trying because my husband is obsessed with it right now.

A twenty-seven-year-old woman wrote:

I enjoy anal sex if I'm prepared for it, and have come once already.

A thirty-one-year-old woman wrote:

I love it, and I think he likes it, too, but not nearly as much as I do. I think he worries about the germ factor too much.

A thirty-three-year-old woman wrote:

I did it once, when I was very drunk.

Need I say that it's a terrible idea to do such things when you're drunk or otherwise incapable of making a rational decision. Not only do you do things you might regret later, but you tend to be careless— and anal sex, when approached carelessly, can be a life sentence.

A thirty-eight-year-old woman wrote:

We have had anal sex on occasion but I have never truly enjoyed it. I think it's just something different that I might learn to enjoy eventually so we persist.

A forty-one-year-old woman has a slightly different slant on anal sex. She wrote:

No. We have tried and it was very painful for me. However, I get very turned on watching anal sex in porn movies.

A forty-three-year-old woman wrote:

I really enjoy it, especially if he talks dirty to me and spanks my ass at the same time. It's such a turn-on to have a hot ass outside that's being fucked on the inside. He has told me that he loves the feeling of my heated buns against his crotch.

A fifty-one-year-old woman wrote:

I originally did it just for him but have since discovered that I really enjoy it. It's a very intense feeling that I never would have guessed I would enjoy.

A fifty-eight-year-old woman wrote:

At first I did it because I knew it was something he wanted to do and I will admit that I was intrigued as well. It wasn't as much fun as I had hoped—in fact it was pretty painful. Since then we've done it a few more times, but I still don't have the "hang" of it. I do have to admit that it turns me on to think about having his cock in my ass. I know he enjoys doing it to me but as yet I haven't "done" it to him. I'm pretty sure he wouldn't enjoy it.

A thirty-two-year-old man wrote:

My wife and I include anal play and intercourse frequently in our lovemaking. My wife loves to use a vibrator on her clit as I fuck her ass from behind and she always has a very intense orgasm. I love to have my wife fuck my ass with a vibrating strap-on dildo. We also love fingering each other's ass during oral sex.

A forty-one-year-old man wrote:

My longtime girlfriend and I only do it a few times a year, I'm sad to say. I don't really know why, since she comes like a bomb that way. I think it would be better for her if she'd just do it rather than worrying about it. Maybe she thinks she shouldn't enjoy it. I don't know.

A forty-two-year-old man wrote:

My current partner won't let me touch her there, and doesn't discuss it.

A previous lady I was with loved digital anal stimulation, and we routinely did it while we were engaged in sex. We tried penile penetration a couple of times, but she said it was just too painful, although we did complete the act, if only for me.

A forty-five-year-old man wrote:

Yes, we do have anal sex, but not frequently. I'm not sure she is very keen on it. I try to be sure she is as comfortable with it as she can be, and I know she appreciates that consideration, but I don't think she gets off on it (yet). For sure, she knows what it does for me since I have the most overwhelmingly powerful orgasms. I really hope she learns to enjoy it, if only half as much as I do.

A forty-seven-year-old man wrote:

We love to rim each other and she loves to fuck my ass with a vibrator.

A fifty-year-old man wrote:

We don't have anal intercourse at all. It's definitely not in the cards for her, and I'm not that interested in trying it.

Occasionally, however, she will gently insert her finger into my ass or rub just around the outside of my anus as we play. Nothing too deep or anything, but that really drives me nuts, and she knows it.

Here's a response from a fifty-six-year-old man who has taken it quite a bit farther. He wrote:

YES [capitals are his]. This is one of the things we have both discovered we like to do that neither of us had done before. Part of our anal sex involves oral stimulation.

I discovered while I was eating her pussy that I enjoyed licking her asshole and she found it wonderful as well. That progressed to making love to her ass with my tongue (actual penetration), which when combined with manual stimulation of her pussy led to her having wonderful orgasms. That eventually led to my fucking her ass.

The other side of the coin has been very interesting also. She has made oral sex so unbelievable because she is so willing to stimulate me in any way possible. Besides taking me fully into her mouth, including continuing while I come and swallowing it (a very new experience for me), she also enjoys licking and sucking on my balls. I have come to the conclusion, and have shared with her, that my balls are the physical equivalent to her breasts. She very much enjoys the physical stimulation I give to her breasts with my mouth and she has translated my feelings to actions on my testicles. She will bathe them with her tongue and very gently put them in her mouth until I am very stimulated and then she will suck on them gently, which is tricky, but when I am very close to coming is wonderful!!! I even have started shaving my pubic hair around my cock and balls to make it more enjoyable for both of us.

Finally, she and I discovered that her licking the area below my balls and before you reach my asshole is very stimulating. She had done that several times to me and one time licked my asshole. I about died and came almost immediately to both our wonder and glee! She has done this several times since and it almost always makes me come. She has also tried to enter me with her tongue but has been unsuccessful *so far*. One of the problems may be relaxing my sphincter. I usually will use my fingers to open her a bit before I can get my tongue inside her. She has wonderful fingernails that are very painful when she has tried stimulating me in the same way. This is one reason I have thought to buy a small dildo for both our pleasure.

A *thirty-one-year-old man wrote:*

The best time we ever had was the night she introduced me to ass fucking. She had done it with a previous boyfriend and had been talking to me about it. I will admit it intrigued me, but we hadn't done anything about it until then.

That evening we got so hot that I decided to let her fuck my ass with a lubed-up toy. I ended up liking it a lot, so now from time to time she straps on a dildo and, while reaching around and stroking my cock, she aggressively fucks me from behind.

A *twenty-seven-year-old woman wrote:*

I think anal sex saved our marriage. It was about a week after I had our first child and, on doctor's orders we were prevented from having real sex for five more weeks. I was so horny though that I begged my husband for anal sex. He had asked to try it before but I never wanted to until then. Well, that was the first time we'd ever done it that way. It felt so good and we each had fabulous climaxes.

A *forty-eight-year-old man wrote:*

Ahh. Anal sex. When I was about twenty-six years old I dated a lady who was divorced and six years older than I was. She was uninhibited in bed, and it seemed that she had already done most everything. I was pretty inexperienced then so it was fantastic learning from her.

She was anally oriented and would have me fingering her ass while she was riding my penis, which I found incredibly exciting. Sometimes I penetrated her ass and fingered her clit. Boy, did she come hard.

Back then I could make it with her before we went out to eat, and come right back and go at it again. When she was on top with my finger(s) in her ass, the feel of her riding up and down on my penis was just indescribable.

I always wanted to try double penetration with two dildos or my cock and a dildo, as I'm sure the feel of two pricks rubbing together in her ass and cunt would have been mind-blowing. Sadly, we broke up before I ever had the chance.

A *thirty-year-old woman wrote:*

I remember my first time, and I will admit that I was drunk. I had a few highballs and, after lots of kissing and touching, my partner tried anal on me. He used lots of lube—I guess he was ready for it—and went really slowly. It took a little while for me to adjust, but then I loved it. He was so gentle and it felt better than vaginal sex.

five

TOYS AND GAMES

PLAYING
WITH TOYS

Do you have a toy box, bag, drawer? Ed and I have toys in several places. I have a vibrator under my bed, at hand when we want it, and we have a bag and a bottom drawer for storing goodies like dildos of various sizes and shapes, different vibrators, dress-up clothes, and lots more.

Ed was the brave one, purchasing our first dildo in a New York City erotic emporium. He says he wasn't nervous—in those days I would have been a wreck. Nowadays, of course, you can shop anonymously on the Internet without fear of embarrassment. And by the way, just browsing together can lead to lots of nights of great sex. Oh, and if you buy something, be sure that, when the item arrives, you have the proper-size batteries handy. There's nothing more frustrating than being really in the mood and finding that you have no AAs in the house.

Ed and I also have a collection of innocent-looking stuff we purchased at the hardware store: lengths of soft rope, heavy chains with padlocks, and several dog and cat collars, which do a great job as wrist and ankle restraints. We also have a few old scarves both for bondage games and for use as blindfolds. Needless to say, this equipment costs a lot less than the equivalent items bought through a catalog or Web site, especially before you know your particular likes and dislikes. It would be a shame to spend fifty dollars for restraints and then discover that you don't enjoy playing as much as you thought you would.

I gather that there are companies that arrange sex-toy parties in your home. They are similar to Tupperware parties and, with a bit of wine and cheese, can be a great deal of fun. I've never been to one but it sounds like a fabulous idea to me.

Let's see what the neighbors like to play with, where they get their toys, and whether they are embarrassed shopping.

A *thirty-eight-year-old woman wrote:*

Because my husband comes very quickly, I need more stimulation than he can provide with his penis for me to reach orgasm. We found that using toys works with me, and allows him to do his thing without feeling he can't satisfy me.

We purchased our first toy from an adult store and hell yes I was mortified! The rest came from the Xandria catalog. Unfortunately, what looks good in the catalog doesn't always work as well as you'd expect.

Too true, and that's the disadvantage of shopping from catalogs and on the Net. Ed and I have several things that looked like a good idea when we ordered them but turned out to be duds. If you buy something that turns out to be a loser, just remember the old axiom. If at first you don't succeed . . .

A *sixty-year-old man wrote:*

We have several cock rings to keep me hard and keep my balls exposed. That way my girlfriend can play with me without my losing my erection or coming too quickly.

A *twenty-one-year-old woman wrote:*

I would like to play with toys but we haven't. Not yet at any rate.

We've talked about it but he's agreed to wait until I'm ready.

My partner recently bought a set of three dildos that I am anticipating adding to our sex life! He just got them for me and he's hidden them away. He's letting me get all worked up using my vivid imagination. I think I'll tell him I'm ready to give them a try. What the hell!!!

A forty-seven-year-old man wrote:

We play with toys maybe once out of every four times we make love. My wife has two vibrators that she likes me to use on her. Also, she likes putting one against my cock while I am in her.

A thirty-two-year-old man wrote:

My wife has come to appreciate a well-used dildo. She realized that she liked coming with my penis inside her but unfortunately, she tends to require a lot of clitoral stimulation (fingers, tongue, or otherwise). Therefore it's easier to bring her pleasure this way.

I bought our toys at an adult store. Embarrassed? Hell no. I love the thought of people thinking, *Wow, he gets to use all this stuff, the lucky bastard.* That was always my attitude when I was buying condoms before my wife and I were married. I'd buy a jumbo box of ribbed ones at Osco and watch the eyes of the high school gal ringing up the order. It was priceless.

A forty-eight-year-old man wrote:

We play with toys often. I had thought about it for a long time before the first time I suggested it and I didn't quite know how to bring it up. Eventually I got a catalog and just said, "I'm game if you are." She was certainly "game." Now I regret all the time I wasted.

A fifty-nine-year-old man wrote:

Not very often, and only when I get the toys out, and get new batteries. I like playing because it's something to prolong sex and a different way to get her excited.

A twenty-year-old bisexual woman wrote:

My boyfriend and I don't own any "proper" sex toys, but we have made do with assorted household objects in the past. Hairbrush handles, an old body spray aerosol, a small jar of massage oil, a tube of vitamin tablets, have all been pressed into service as dildos.

We particularly play at times when we can't have sex. Since I'm not on the pill or anything we resort to other methods of sexual satisfaction when I am particularly fertile.

I do have one embarrassing "toy" story, though. In my previous relationship, this one with a woman, my girlfriend and I were quite adventurous. We didn't own any sex toys but I remember I once bought a cucumber, and at an appropriate moment asked my girlfriend to fuck me with it. She laughed heartily, and eventually said she would but only if I could ask her with a straight face. So with a barely held poker face, I said, "Please fuck me with a cucumber!" Amazingly, this turned her on, and we had some of the best sex of our lives. That was eighteen months ago now, but it's still a vivid memory.

A thirty-three-year-old woman wrote:

I never played with toys before my current boyfriend but he is wonderfully uninhibited. He's got me doing things I never would have before. He likes to use toys like a big dildo and two different vibrators, one electric and one with batteries. He either does things himself or he watches me play with the toys while he masturbates. Sometimes he tells me "exactly" what to do with the vibrators and that turns us both on.

A fifty-one-year-old female wrote:

My husband and I use toys every time we have sex. We have a vibrating egg that goes inside my vagina when we are doing sixty-nine or when we have anal sex. I remember when we bought it. We shopped together at an adult sex-toy store and I was mortified. He made the purchase while I pretended to be engrossed by looking at video titles. I was a bit hesitant about playing at first, and for a long time I didn't use anything when I was alone. Now, however, if he's away and I'm by myself and horny, I bring out the toy bag.

A forty-seven-year-old woman wrote:

I love to play with dildos, chains, ropes, blindfolds, vibrators, feathers, candles, whatever! If you want to play with toys but never have, just suggest it. If a partner says that he or she isn't comfortable with it you have to respect that. If he or she isn't comfortable, then it is not going to make the lovemaking enjoyable.

A thirty-six-year-old woman suggested:

It helps to introduce sex toys when you have driven your partner crazy and they are so horny they are begging for you to do anything to get them off. Then show them a new toy. For me, I was never embarrassed to go to the sex store. Why should I be? I am horny for my husband and I love games. If you are shy, order online, naked if you want.

A thirty-one-year-old man wrote:

I have tried every method I can think of to introduce toys to our lovemaking, but she is staunchly opposed to it. It makes me sad.

A twenty-five-year-old woman wrote:

Now we use toys most of the time my husband and I make love. At first they scared him, and when we bought our first dildo it remained in the store bag for several weeks. Then one evening while making love he said, "Get the bag." I asked whether he was sure and he said, "Hurry before I change my mind." Now he is the one reaching for the bag on his own.

A twenty-seven-year-old woman wrote:

Sadly, my husband and I have never played with toys together, but I have just gotten a toy for when I'm masturbating. I would have been embarrassed to go and pick one out, or order one I think, but a very sophisticated girlfriend of mine knew I was curious, got one, and gave it to me. I'm very grateful to her now.

A *twenty-eight-year-old woman wrote:*

My husband and I have a variety of toys. We use a regular vaginal vibrator during oral sex and sometimes we use a small anal one for added stimulation. I have to say that sex got ten times better after we brought toys into our sex life. We became closer and were able to open up a little more freely on what we wanted sexually.

A *thirty-year-old woman wrote:*

The silver bullet is great. Just rest it on your pubic bone while having intercourse. It relays the vibrations through your pussy to his cock. Yum yum.

A *thirty-four-year-old woman wrote:*

We have a penis-shaped vibrator but I like to use it as a dildo without the vibrations. We also have some dice that have sexual things on them so that when you toss them they instruct you to do something naughty; powders and oils that are edible; and a pair of ben wa balls.

Ladies, if you want to tell a man you want to play, just do it. Most men seem to be turned on by a woman who enjoys toys.

A *forty-three-year-old woman wrote:*

Although my boyfriend's a bit shy, when we first met I made it known that I'm slightly kinky and enjoyed all kinds of games. I bought a penis whip and nipple clamps and kept them hidden away until I thought he was ready to play. He found them one night and knew that I wanted them used on me.

He was a bit hesitant at first but I told him gently exactly what I wanted. He told me later that my talking made it lots easier for him because that way he knew exactly what I expected. In the future I'd like to try soft restraints, leather gloves (for spanking my ass), soft whips that sting but don't hurt too much, clit clips, and an anal vibrator to put in my ass while he fucks my pussy and bites my nipples.

A fifty-one-year-old woman wrote:

We used a blindfold once. It was a lot of fun but sadly I've never seen it again. I think it would be fun to experiment with other things. I've always had a fantasy of his tying me up and "having his way" with me but I don't think he's interested in that one.

A fifty-eight-year-old woman wrote:

We use toys a lot! We like to play with vibrators and other forms of dildo-type toys, as well as silk scarves, feathers, flavored lotions, whipped cream, etc. Anything that stimulates the senses adds to the excitement of our sex play and lovemaking. We both also love lingerie, and I enjoy dressing up in outfits that I know turn him on. I'm even thinking about buying a wig in case he wants to make love to a blonde!

In the beginning with my current partner it sort of just happened. I've always had my private little toy chest, and when he bought me the first of many vibrators, I knew it was time to show him the other fun things I own. I've even made the leap to getting him some "guy" toys. So far he isn't having as much fun with them as I do with mine, but we're still working on it.

In the early days I shopped through the mail using advertisements I found in the back of magazines. Now I use the Internet, and occasionally go to an "adult" store. I was embarrassed at first, convinced everyone in town knew because I was sure that the postman would tell everyone that I received "plain brown wrappers." Now it's sort of funny to get advertisements that say SEXU-ALLY EXPLICIT MATERIALS on the outside of the envelope. I guess we don't worry about those things as much anymore, but I'm still embarrassed to visit some of the "adult" stores, where I have to purchase things like split-crotch panties from a real live person.

As for approaching someone new with your love of toys, not

everyone is open to this. You just sort of have to wait and see, or broach it very carefully. Thank heaven for an adventurous, enthusiastic lover!

A *thirty-two-year-old bisexual man wrote:*

My wife and I often include toys in our love play. We have vibrators, clitoral stimulators, anal dildos, and some restraints and blindfolds. We use them primarily as an extra stimulus during foreplay or intercourse, but sometimes my wife will tie me down and masturbate with her vibrator while I'm "forced" to watch. Her favorite vibrator is called the Techno Rabbit. It has moving beads inside a vibrating, rotating shaft with a protruding clitoral vibrator. It almost makes me obsolete, but I enjoy stroking myself as I watch her launch herself into orgasmic orbit.

We started using toys to allow ourselves the opportunity to play in new ways and in new places. The first toy we ever used was a basic bullet-shaped vibrator I got from a mail-order company. I got it for her—she was then my fiancée—so she could use it on herself in the car on long trips. She enjoyed it so much that she got me to use it on her as she went down on me. It was poorly made and didn't last more than a couple of months, so when the time came to replace it, I talked her into going to an upscale sex shop to pick out another one.

She was very nervous, but very intrigued by all the different types of sex toys available. She was amazed at the variety and had a hard time choosing, but since she was embarrassed to be in a sex shop, she quickly picked out a more realistic-looking vibrator and made me pay for it. Let me say that not only was she embarrassed, she was also very aroused. When we got in the car, she quickly opened the box and examined her new treasure. She was so excited, she made me pull into the nearest convenience store to buy batteries and practically wore those out on the ride home.

Now we go to the adult store every couple of months and

make a date out of it. She has gotten over her shyness, and eagerly and closely examines each product on the shelf. She really gets excited and never forgets to get the batteries.

A *thirty-two-year-old man wrote:*

My wife already had a few toys from her single days but she was embarrassed about it. One evening she made a joke about them to test the waters. I let her know really quickly that I was eager to play and we've been enjoying ourselves ever since.

In the future, I would like to try a hands-free sleeve by the same company that makes the Sybian, or maybe one of those multi-thousand-dollar lifelike dolls. Maybe someday.

For those who might not know, a hands-free sleeve is a cylindrical vibrator that fits over the penis and a Sybian is a very expensive vibrating dildo that women can mount for sexual pleasure.

A *thirty-six-year-old man wrote:*

My wife had a vibrator before we met and sometimes I use it on her or she uses it while I watch. It is nice to see her wild with lust from the little buzzer

If I were trying to bring toys into a new relationship I might ask if she had ever used any. If she said yes, then I'd ask whether she still had them. With several old girlfriends, when we were just beginning to make love after dates I brought a little vibrator with me and introduced it when the woman was really hot. Most of the women loved it, although afterward a few felt as if they had been tricked. Of course, when I agreed and said I wouldn't use my little toy anymore, they were quick to change their minds and allow me to do it to them again . . . soon!

A *forty-five-year-old man wrote:*

My wife and I have a number of dildos, vibrators, anal probes, soft-lined wrist and ankle bracelets with rope for bondage, a blindfold, a spatula for light spanking. I also made a set of adjustable nipple clamps out of clothes pegs, based on illustrations from an Internet site.

I think we "matured" into them. I wouldn't have thought of such a thing in the early years of our relationship but as time passed we wanted to experiment a little. I think the Internet and access to erotica that described their use inspired me considerably.

I buy my toys at a typical adult video/sex-toy novelty shop. It's difficult to remain nervous since the woman who owns it is so helpful and matter-of-fact, you'd think you were buying a carton of eggs from her.

A forty-five-year-old man wrote:

When I wanted to try toys the first time, I told my wife that I had read that Dr. Ruth recommended it, and she agreed to give it a try, even though she was apprehensive at first. Since then we've played more and more. Now I don't have any problem buying toys. I am an adult and am proud of my sexuality. . . .

A fifty-year-old man wrote:

I bought a small four-inch vibrator a few years ago to experiment on my wife as a foreplay toy and we still use it occasionally. When she is in the mood it drives her nuts, but she fights it. I think the whole idea frightens her—maybe she thinks it's dirty or something.

A seventy-seven-year-old man wrote:

We sometimes play with toys as part of foreplay. We have both a vibrator and a vibrating dildo. My wife is pretty subtle when she is interested (smile)! She indicates that she wants to use them by simply reaching across me to the nightstand to get one or both. She controls the vibrator on her clitoris and nipples while I use the dildo in her vagina.

A twenty-five-year-old woman wrote:

My husband doesn't like to put his fingers into my pussy after he comes inside me. He says it's gross so I bought a dildo to help when I haven't come yet.

There are only two stores where I live to get stuff like that. One is gross, with dirty old men playing with themselves in the back room. I went there once and they made me feel disgusting. The other is run by a cute little old lady and it's clean. She's never made me feel like a pervert or embarrassed about going in there so I go there a lot. She also has sexy lingerie in plus sizes!

A thirty-year-old woman wrote:

No toys yet. My boyfriend is still in the closet about sex and that sucks! I plan to have a sex-toy party soon. He will be shy about it, but we will have lots of fun. Eventually.

A forty-six-year-old man wrote:

When my wife was having trouble getting to climax I used a vibrator on her and she still enjoys it a lot!

A thirty-one-year-old man wrote:

Long ago I developed a fetish for chastity belts. I bought one and asked my wife to play with me and at first she refused. After several months, however, she gave it a try, but it still took a while before she got comfortable with the idea.

During June 1998 she had to go out of town for a week to attend a conference. She shyly suggested that I wear the chastity belt while she was gone and I eagerly agreed. That week was a wonderful dichotomy of sexual arousal and frustration.

The night she got back I was drooling all over myself in anticipation of a night of great sex. Unfortunately for me, the flight was somewhat bumpy and she arrived feeling a bit airsick. She did not offer to end my frustration but instead suggested we get a good night's sleep. I spent the night snuggled up next to her with my caged member throbbing for release. It was wonderful torture, just what I had in mind when I bought the thing.

The next morning she unlocked the belt and we took a long

hot shower, then hit the bedroom for an all-day sexcapade. What made it so great was the feeling that she had accepted my fantasy and was apparently taking pleasure from sharing it with me. Unfortunately, that was the last time she was interested in that fantasy. Maybe . . .

A thirty-six-year-old man wrote:

The best sex I ever had was with a girl I met a long time ago. She was so open to everything I liked and wanted to try new things. We used toys and nipple clamps and, well, everything. We even watched X-rated films together. She was just so open about her sexuality.

A forty-eight-year-old man wrote:

Recently something new happened for my girlfriend and me. We bought our first vibrator and took it home to try out. My girlfriend undressed, got on the bed, and I took the vibrator and began rubbing her breasts, legs, and nipples. I watched her nipples get stiff as I massaged them with the toy.

She spread her legs real wide and I put the vibrator on her vaginal lips. Fluid was starting to flow and she reached down with her fingertips and gently pulled her outer lips open so I could see the nub of her erect clitoris. I put the vibrator against it and she moaned softly. There was juice all over her vulva as the toy hummed. She was bucking her hips as the stimulation reached its peak.

Not everyone who responded was interested in playing with toys. A forty-year-old woman wrote:

I never played and won't. Our own body parts are toys enough!

That just about says it, so consider your partner's wishes whatever you decide to do.

DO YOU AND YOUR PARTNER PLAY PRETEND GAMES?

Pretend games. What do they add to the bedroom, you might wonder. Actually playing pretend games allows both partners the freedom to do something or be someone they might not be as comfortable doing without the camouflage of another persona. For example, have you ever wanted to be dominant? Be the pirate, the strict teacher with an unruly student, or the prison guard with access to the prisoners of the opposite sex? How about being a police officer? Have you ever wanted your partner to take advantage of you in a situation over which you have no control? Be pretend-hypnotized or asleep when the burglar invades your bedroom? Got the idea?

When I asked specifically whether anyone had played pirate, doctor, or prison guard, I got a few new ideas. In addition, one woman wrote that she had played a French maid, a nurse, a belly dancer, a stripper, and, a new one to me, Santa's helper. All delicious scenarios. I also asked how the respondent would react if his or her partner answered the door dressed as a police officer or a doctor. Lots of folks answered, "Wowee," or words to that effect. If you've never considered it, maybe it's time.

Ed and I love playing games in the bedroom. I'm the "bad little girl" and he's only doing things for my own good, to teach me a lesson. Or he's being invaded from behind while his penis is inside me. There are just too many variations to go into here. Let's just say it's wonderful!

What do your neighbors play?

A sixty-eight-year-old man wrote:

> I'd like to play games and my wife has said that she wants to be tied up sometime. Playing a doctor game and tying her up would be exciting as can be.

A forty-one-year-old woman wrote:

> My partner and I bought a pirate story kit once and even got a hat to go with it, but so far we haven't used it. I would like to try some fantasy and role-playing adventures, but at this point in our relationship, my partner and I seem to be too inhibited to try it.

Okay, why haven't you played? Is it the risk that prevents you from something that might prove to be so mutually enjoyable? If so, I understand. There is a bit of risk. *What will he or she think of me if I suggest something a bit off center?* You might try the idea of bookmarking that I discussed in the introduction. Use some of the letters in this or other chapters. Think of all the nights of great sex you might be missing and do something about it. It's never too late to give one—or more—a try.

A thirty-three-year-old woman wrote:

> I've never played games, but my partner would love to do this. I guess I would like to also if it weren't for my weight holding me back.

This gives me a place to climb up on my soapbox and rant a bit, so hang on. Ladies, what are we doing to ourselves and what pleasures are we forgoing by worrying about our looks, especially our weight? We are sold a bill of goods every time we open a magazine or turn on our TV set. We aren't lovable (notice I didn't say *beautiful* but *lovable*) if we're not model-slim with clear skin, glorious hair, and the right makeup. Sorry, but I have one word for all that. Bullshit! I usually don't use such strong language, but I can't help it.

I understand that we, as women, are bombarded with all the nonsense, and I, too, fall into the trap. I could stand to lose some weight, as most of us could. So what? Ed doesn't care, and your partner probably doesn't care either. If he had the choice, he would want you warm, willing, and playful in his bed rather than spending time waiting for you to feel better about yourself. Ladies, think hard. Realize that you're not only denying yourself, you're denying your partner—and he's the one you're trying to please. Let him enjoy you as you are.

A *twenty-one-year-old woman wrote:*

I've never played any games but I definitely want to. Allowing me to act out some of my fantasies would definitely make our sex lives much more exciting. And if he met me in "costume" it would be an automatic turn-on. I would immediately be excited and anticipate what would happen after I walked in the door. I'd probably rip his clothes off and start in right then!

A *fifty-two-year-old man wrote:*

My wife and I love to role-play in our relationship. Some of our favorite characters are: Candy, a professional escort, Angel, a much younger novice prostitute/escort, the Schoolgirl (self-explanatory), and the Mistress. Sometimes I play Harry, a man who frequently comes to view Candy's peep show. It always leads to a night of great sex.

A *fifty-four-year-old man wrote:*

My last lover was a pagan and fantasized being taken by Pan deep in the forest. I brought her out to the woods behind her aunt's house one night and wore suction-cup horns while I "raped" her. At first I was doing it for her but in the end I don't know who enjoyed it more.

A forty-seven-year-old man wrote:

My girlfriend likes to dress up like a little girl and be taught all about sex. I, too, dress up as a baby at times so I can suckle her hot little titties.

A forty-eight-year-old man wrote:

My wife enjoys it when I make up stories about her getting laid. She likes me to fantasize about very large penises or talk about her being seduced interracially. She also likes to have me make up stories that involve soft-core rape scenes, where she is almost a willing participant. Another favorite is a tale in which she is attending some function alone and gets picked up by a guy and taken to his room where she would get screwed.

A seventy-seven-year-old man wrote:

My lady and I just sat down and talked about this section (yes, she's been watching what I've been typing). While I've never, to my memory, ever thought of playing pretend games, she is telling me that she has. This is her "pretend."

She would like me to pretend I am her gynecologist and have me do a vaginal exam on her. As she says, "I'd like you to really open me up, maybe with a speculum or something, and look inside me." So I guess in the near future, I'm going to play doctor.

If my partner met me at the door dressed as a doctor with a stethoscope hanging around her neck I would confirm that I had an "appointment," complain of some problem with my penis, and immediately strip and prepare to be examined.

It seems that just filling out this survey expanded the sexual horizons of at least one couple. Fabulous!

A forty-seven-year-old man wrote:

Our favorite character is "Debbie," the cheerleader from *Debbie Does Dallas.* She dresses up, then does me.

I like her to dress up as a schoolgirl, too. She has a short pleated school-type skirt to which she adds a white blouse and patent-leather shoes. We're still developing other characters. Recently I asked her to dress up as a "whore," a real slutty look. She hasn't done it yet, but eventually . . .

A forty-eight-year-old man wrote:

My favorite game is having my wife pretend to be a hooker. I play picked her up several times in a hotel bar. I don't think anyone else at the bar knew we were married and, to tell the truth, I didn't feel married.

A fifty-nine-year-old man wrote:

Several months ago my wife planned to meet me at the door "dressed" in only Saran wrap, but I got home an hour early. When she told me how disappointed she was, I was so intrigued that I helped make her a Saran wrap outfit. It consisted of a skirt, one width of wrap tall, and a separate top of wrap folded in half.

Once, years ago, she met me at the airport wearing just a teddy under her coat. That was super.

A thirty-one-year-old man wrote:

I'd love to play employer/employee. I'd be my lady's employee and get chewed out by her, then I'd have to do what she wants in order to keep my job.

A fifty-one-year-old woman wrote:

If my husband met me at the front door in some sort of costume, I would cream my pants, especially if he was a police officer with cuffs who wanted to frisk me. Wooo Hoooo!

A twenty-five-year-old woman wrote:

There was one time I told my boyfriend that I have always wanted to play little girl and make love on a slide. We just happened to be at the park, so we went to the new slide gym and proceeded. It was dewy and kinda cool outside and extremely exhilarating.

A thirty-one-year-old woman wrote:

My favorite role was playing the World War II prisoner of war while my husband was the Nazi interrogator, torturing me for information. Mmm. I have a very high tolerance for torture!!

A thirty-four-year-old woman wrote:

I like to pretend that my boyfriend and I have never been together before and that my folks might catch us. Then he touches me with his penis and nothing else.

A forty-three-year-old woman wrote:

My hubby and I have played a game of my being a bad girl and needing a good hard fucking up my ass and a hard spanking. This game *always* gets my pussy hot and wet.

I'd absolutely love it if he answered the door dressed as a police officer, handcuffed me, and forced me to bend over the couch while he spanked my ass with his leather-gloved hand and occasionally slapped my clit until I came.

A forty-five-year-old woman wrote:

One of my lovers was an officer in the navy. It was the most wonderful turn-on to see him come to the door in his uniform. We didn't have to *play* at it. He was my officer and gentleman or, more wonderfully, not such a gentleman.

A fifty-eight-year-old woman wrote:

Although we like the idea, we've never really gotten into role playing. I think it would be great. I'd really like to have the time and costumes to "act out" one of our fantasies, and to provide each other with that kind of pleasure. Oh baby, baby! Let's go for it!!!

A sixty-two-year-old woman wrote:

I've pretended that I was being fucked by another couple while my husband was fucking me. I pretended my own fingers were the woman's!

A twenty-seven-year-old man wrote:

A few years ago my partner and I pretended that she was my girlfriend's cousin, age sixteen or so. Sometimes she'd seduce me and other times I'd seduce her. Breaking down taboo barriers was hot. Another time my partner dressed me perfectly as a female and I played her lesbian lover.

A thirty-year-old man wrote:

I would like to play student and have my wife be the teacher. She could educate me about my cock, teach me how to make myself come, and then give me several lessons about her cunt and asshole.

A thirty-two-year-old man wrote:

My wife and I have just started to dabble in role-playing fantasies. She has played nurse, which is a turn-on for me. I would also love her to dress up as a policewoman and totally dominate me.

I am trying to get a feel for what she would like so I can surprise her one night. Prison guard sounds like a fun one. And if I walked into the house to see my wife in a police uniform holding a nightstick, my hard-on would be trying to rip through my pants before I got the door closed behind me.

A thirty-six-year-old man wrote:

Maybe we could meet in a bar and I could pick her up as if we are just meeting for the first time. Or maybe there could be a bit of a chase through the woods, ending in bending her over a stump or something—you know—sort of a simulated rape thing.

A forty-year-old man wrote:

My wife and I like to pretend that I'm her hired hand and I perform "chores" around her body. Sometimes I like to pretend that I'm her love slave. She wins me in a card game from another woman and first I show her what the other woman liked, then she shows me what she wants.

A forty-two-year-old man wrote:

My girlfriend pretends to be a senior office manager interviewing young male candidates for a job. She has me dress in a suit and disrobe at her will. If my cock gets hard, she gets angry and won't let me have the job. When she wants it hard, I have to get erect without touching myself, then she directs me to do various things to her: kiss her breasts, feel up her skirt, caress her feet. I must stay hard all the time. Fucking is not usually part of the fantasy for her but we always do afterward! Mostly it's just the control over these young men and their firm bodies.

One forty-five-year-old man would love to play but needs some guidance from his lady. He wrote:

I can't say that we have played pretend games in a really overt way with dressing up, props, etc. I think perhaps we are both too inhibited and too self-conscious—at least so far. During passionate lovemaking I have suggested that my partner imagine I am someone else, and to a limited extent to imagine we are somewhere else under other circumstances. It did seem to add spice. It could also pave the way to fantasy becoming reality.

I think role playing would be interesting to pursue. I would particularly like it if she would give me some idea of who or where she would like to be and how she would want the game to go. I have some inkling of where she might be with this, based on "favorite" stories she marked off in one of your books (Nice Couples Do). I haven't had her read a lot of erotica, but I think it's a very good way to help someone identify what turns them on when they may not feel comfortable saying what that is.

Here's an idea for you. Lie in bed and start an erotic story. Set the scene and describe the people. Then ask her how the next part might go. Alternate paragraphs to ease the way and see what she comes up with. You'll find out quite quickly what excites her.

A twenty-five-year-old woman wrote:

I would like to go to a bar, pretend I don't know him, and "pick him up." I would love the feeling that everyone around would know what would happen. There's a feeling of control and power.

If he answered the door dressed like a police officer I'd probably chuckle, but then I would say, "Are you going to frisk me, Officer? Have I been bad? Are you going to handcuff me now and show me how bad I've been?" Then hopefully he'd push me up against the wall and take over.

A twenty-five-year-old woman wrote:

It's the rapist-and-victim–type scenario that really turns me on. It's the only way I can get my husband to be dominant with me and I love when he gets really forceful.

A thirty-year-old woman wrote:

I've never played pretend. Although I really want to, I am shy for that. I would love to be cuffed by a cop and then fucked. Or be hosed by a fireman (smile).

A thirty-nine-year-old bisexual woman wrote:

Okay, you asked for it. Here's how my role-playing session would go.

I am a prison inmate being taken to the female warden to become her sex slave. When I refuse, she ties me up, whips me, and rapes me with her strap-on dildo, taking me whenever and however she wants until I am hers and will do as she wishes.

A forty-six-year-old man wrote:

I don't know how I would react if my wife answered the door dressed up in some way. She has, however, answered the door naked and ready to go at it! That was wonderful!

A sixty-two-year-old man wrote:

The closest we come to pretend is lingerie. I like sexy high-class sheer and lacy items: thongs, body stockings, camisoles, and stay-up hose with lace tops, the kind of lingerie one sees in fashion magazines, not at Frederick's of Hollywood. My wife wears such things for me at special times, but does not like it for everyday wear. My lady in sheer lingerie turns me on every time. Her collection is extensive and expensive . . . and yes, I buy some of it for her. She likes me to wear tight Jockey shorts, sometimes, when we make love so that she can peel them off me when she is ready.

A twenty-two-year-old man wrote:

One of the best nights my wife and I ever spent was when she asked me to pretend that she was a virgin and force her into having sex. I am not usually a very aggressive or forceful person, but role playing enabled me to satisfy this need. She kept saying that she didn't want to do it, and that it was wrong. I just forced her legs apart, and rammed my cock up inside her. I kept telling her what a filthy whore she was, and that a dirty little bitch like her couldn't help herself. I fucked her really hard, and we both came with screams. That was a really satisfying, yet scary experience.

A thirty-nine-year-old man wrote:

I remember the first girl I ever had sex with. We had become lovers and she was very adventurous, willing and anxious to do new things. I had told her that I wanted us to make love and talk dirty during sex. We could say anything we wanted so long as we understood it meant nothing. *She agreed!*

We both stripped and started. I pretended that she was a nymph and loved being forced to pleasure her partner. We began by kissing and fondling one another. I would call her a cheap slut and tell her to suck my nipples and stroke my dick. I would call her my little cheap bitch and tell her that I would never fuck her if she didn't do what I told her. She was great and slipped right into the role. (She had become one of the best cocksuckers I have ever been with and she blew my balls off that night.) We traded places and to my surprise she was better at the part than I had been. She would tell me to suck her tits and then laugh at me and tell me that she thought I could suck her harder than that. I found out that night that she enjoyed very aggressive sex. I loved the way she would call me bastard, and motherfucker. I enjoyed telling her how good it was to have a slut to fuck.

FANTASY AND REALITY

Threesomes, Watching and Being Watched,
Control, Pain, Homosexuality

DO YOU FANTASIZE?

A h, fantasies. Most of us have them, and many keep it secret from their partners. Of those who answered the questions in my survey, 57% of the men and 51% of the women fantasize during sex, and 88% of the men and 69% of the women fantasize at other times. I'm surprised the percentages are that low.

Should you fantasize? There are no "shoulds" about it. It's normal and natural and you really can't control where your dreams take you, during sex or at other times. Of those who responded to the survey, 75% of the men and 53% of the women have dreamed about making love to another person. Maybe it's a film star, maybe the guy next door or the gal at the office. Have folks acted on those fantasies? Probably not. But they are fun, nonetheless.

Sharing a fantasy can be a wonderful thing. Maybe it's telling tales in the dark, or perhaps the two of you can actually figure a way to act it out together. However, it's also possible that you prefer to keep your fantasies private. That's fine, too. I have a few that even Ed doesn't know about. Somehow discussing them takes the delicious edge off, and I don't want to do that. Oh, and Ed has one

or two as well. Am I curious? Sure, but I won't ask. He is entitled
to his private worlds, too.

Here's a pretty common fantasy.

A *forty-five-year-old man wrote:*

I fantasize about the women in *Playboy* or *Penthouse* magazine.
I'd like one of them to decorate my cock, and I her pussy with
whipped cream and chocolate syrup. She'd then slowly lick every
bit of it while I do the same to her. When we're both squeaky
clean she'd straddle me and fuck me as I lie there sucking on her
nipples. Then she would dismount and nuzzle between my legs,
sucking my cock slowly, taking its entire length into her mouth
while fondling my balls. She would slowly lick the length of my
stiff cock until I come, and she would swallow it all.

Others dreamed about soft breezes on hot summer nights, sandy
beaches lit only by moonlight, turquoise water and . . . well, you
get the picture. There are an almost infinite variety of "traditional
dreams."

Most of the more off-center fantasies fit into one of the five cat-
egories and are contained in the sections that follow: threesomes,
watching and being watched, control, pain, and homosexuality. A
few, however, don't fit into any specific category.

A *thirty-one-year-old man wrote:*

I love to fantasize about size differences, where I'm only about
two or three feet tall and the woman is full height. It's more of a
giantess or shrinking fantasy than an age thing. I just love the
idea of her being really big so I get to play around on larger
breasts or lick a big pussy or fuck a big, firm ass.

A *fifty-one-year-old man wrote:*

My wife is very loving but a very proper schoolteacher. I dream
about one of her former students coming back to thank her for
tutoring him. I fantasize about her with her dress pulled open,

her very white Irish body stretched back on her desk, crying out in joyful orgasm as a young black man fucks her with abandon.

A *fifty-eight-year-old woman* wrote:

This is really "outside the box" as the saying goes but here it is. I've read a few stories about women and their pets that have interested and frightened me at the same time. The idea of owning a dog, or cat, that could provide that little bit of oral pleasure when I'm all alone is tantalizing, but so off limits I don't know how to think about it. I'm afraid, it's a little scary, and perhaps a little perverted. Guess I'll just keep it to myself.

Some who wrote had secret thoughts about deeply taboo topics—sex with someone underage, sex with a family member, and, like this woman, sex with an animal. A few mentioned urine. Fantasies are private thoughts and, as I said earlier, neither good nor bad. As with the writer of this fantasy, they can scare us, but they are what they are. This woman wouldn't dare act out her dream, and only actions are *good* or *bad*. If you have an unusual fantasy, enjoy it. Let it scare you in a delicious way, and let it tantalize you as well.

HAVE YOU EVER FANTASIZED ABOUT A THREESOME?

One of the more common fantasies is the threesome—or four-some—or moresome. Of the people who responded, 71% of the men and 61% of the women had fantasies of (or had acted out) threesomes. Let's see what they said.

A *twenty-one-year-old woman* wrote:

I have actually thought about a threesome with my ex-husband and his brother, one in my pussy, the other in my mouth. I've thought about my current partner and his friend, same circumstances. I have also thought about a threesome with me, my boyfriend, and my best girlfriend. Never having been with a woman in any way before, I think I would be hesitant, but would love to see what it is like to be with a woman—particularly my best girlfriend. I would want her to play with me and both of us to play with my boyfriend.

A *forty-seven-year-old man* wrote:

It would be kind of fun and sexy to climb on one girl, make love for a while, then move to her friend and screw her for a while. It would be really great if the two of them went down on me. First I would be in one mouth while the other licked my balls and ass, then they would change places. There would also be lots of touching and caressing.

A *twenty-two-year-old man* wrote:

I dream about threesomes often. It would involve my partner and either another woman or another man. For the woman, I dream about a particularly attractive female friend of my partner's whom she has admitted she fancies. I would love to either watch them or join in. My biggest fantasy would be to fuck one woman while being fucked up the ass by another woman with a strap-on or by a man.

A *thirty-three-year-old woman* wrote:

I've always wondered what it would be like to be with another woman, and my partner says that he has always fantasized about being with me and another woman. Haven't done it, but I can imagine the two of us together with another woman. He would watch us together while he stroked his cock and then he'd join in, letting the other woman suck his cock while he sucked and licked my pussy.

A *fifty-one-year-old woman* wrote:

I've often fantasized of being with two men, sucking one while the other fucks me, in the ass preferably. I want to use a strap-on on a man, to fuck him, pound into him, make him scream in blissful surrender.

I also fantasize about being in a relationship with two gay men. I want to show both that I can suck and receive and give anal sex as well as any man, then want both to tell me, that yes, fucking me is very good.

A *forty-seven-year-old woman* wrote:

They would both be my servants, my love slaves, and do everything I tell them to do, and make me come many many times.

A thirty-two-year-old man wrote:

I would like to try a threesome with a couple I don't really know and would not have to see too much afterward to avoid awkward feelings. I would also like to have a threesome with my girlfriend and her best friend.

A thirty-nine-year-old man wrote:

I dream about my wife and me with another man. I would love it to be with someone we both know and trust. It's pleasure, sex, and just fucking, not anything to tear us apart. I would love for it to be with someone she picks out, maybe someone with whom she had already been having an affair.

A forty-year-old man wrote:

I fantasize about my wife being loved by a couple of men or more, with me either participating or just watching. I think that it would be tremendously pleasurable for her. I don't see this ever being acted out because of the difficulty of finding the other players to participate when we want, yet not wanting them to be involved afterward. It also must not create misunderstandings or unintended consequences between myself and my wife.

A forty-five-year-old man wrote:

I have fantasies about threesomes, with nobody in particular. A blonde and a brunette would be nice. We'd try lots of different positions, play orally, and I'd please both at the same time. I'd fuck one while the other fucks her and then me with a strap-on. One of them would suck my cock while I eat her pussy and the other girl would suck my balls and probe my ass with her finger. The possibilities are endless!

A twenty-five-year-old woman wrote:

I would love to try two things. First I'd like to be able to perform oral sex while having the other guy fuck me, and second be vaginally and anally fucked at the same time.

A twenty-five-year-old woman wrote:

Threesomes? No, never. I get too jealous and I know my fiancé gets really jealous as well.

A thirty-eight-year-old woman wrote:

Well, sometimes my dream includes someone I know, and sometimes it's with an anonymous stranger. Sometimes the dream is about me and two men, sometimes about me, a woman, and a man, and sometimes it's about me and two women. That last one makes for really wet dreams.

A sixty-two-year-old man wrote:

I dream about being with my wife and a petite lady I know who fascinates me. I would love to see her naked or nearly so. Nothing too exotic, just lots of oral give and take between the ladies and myself and then they take turns, one getting screwed and the other on my face.

A fifty-six-year-old man wrote:

We both have discussed having a threesome with a very close, attractive female friend of my wife's who "interests" both of us.
However, we agree that what we have is special and is not to be shared. I think that performance anxieties would make it a disaster for me anyway.

A twenty-three-year-old woman wrote:

I fantasize about being worshiped by two men, men who only want my pleasure and don't care about their own release. They are so totally excited by me that they can hardly contain themselves. I have never told my husband because I'm afraid that he would be a little hurt, and feel insecure.

A *twenty-seven-year-old woman* wrote:

I have a fantasy also about tying my husband up, and then having another woman join us. Both of us would kneel by his face so he could look up and see our fingers moving in and out of each other's pussies, and licking each other's nipples.

Then one of us would ride his tongue while the other rides his cock. Afterward, we would continue pleasuring each other while he is helpless to touch us. I would act it out if I got the chance, but I'd rather not have my husband know I've thought about it.

A *fifty-eight-year-old woman* wrote:

Sometimes my lover and I pretend that we are having a ménage à trois with our toys. As I suck my lover's cock, he'll tell me about the stranger who is going to fuck me while he teases me with a dildo or vibrator. If I close my eyes I can envision this stranger and imagine a second set of hands on me as our love play continues.

What a delicious way to have a threesome with only the two of you participating. Here's another:

A *forty-two-year-old man* wrote:

I love to tell fantasies to my wife during foreplay. I'll say, for example, that I wonder what one of her work colleagues is like in bed. I ask my wife whether this woman's nipples are small and bright pink or large and dark, or whether she thinks the woman shaves her pussy. It never fails to get my wife and me really hot. Sometimes I'll say a friend (I'll pick someone we both know) is watching us fuck. I'll say he or she is sitting in the corner of the room playing with him- or herself and I'll describe exactly what's happening.

A *thirty-two-year-old man* wrote:

My favorite fantasy involves my wife and me having dinner at another couple's house. Everyone is wearing sexy, revealing clothing and innocently flirting with each other.

As the wine and conversation loosen us up, light flirting touches begin and the sexual tension increases. As I lean close to the other man's wife and listen to her talk while inhaling her intoxicating perfume, I notice the husband lightly caressing my wife's ass. His wife notices also and gently licks my earlobe, which causes me to gasp.

Everyone smiles nervously at each other and my wife looks to me for some sort of sign as the other man's touches turn to caresses. As she stares, my wife sees the other woman's hand sneak around in front of me and lightly rub my crotch. I watch my wife's eyes as she stares intently at the hand moving up and down. Soon I succumb to the pleasure of this woman's caress.

My wife slowly approaches, opens my zipper, and pulls my straining prick free. She places the other woman's hand on my cock and helps her slowly stroke my erection. My wife sticks her tongue in my mouth as I raise the back of her dress in invitation to the man across the room. He steps up behind my wife and grinds his hard cock between her naked ass cheeks. The action that follows changes depending on my mood.

Some of those who wrote told about a three- or moresome they had actually been part of.

A *thirty-one-year-old man wrote:*

I've already tried a threesome and it worked out really badly. It was with my girlfriend's friend "Tiffany." I could tell that my girlfriend was a bit hurt by me having fun with someone else and I can understand her feelings. I'd go nuts watching another man have her. We don't do those things anymore and I find that it left such a bad taste that I don't fantasize about it anymore the way I used to.

A *thirty-eight-year-old bisexual woman wrote:*

The best sex I ever had was as part of a threesome—my husband, my girlfriend, and me. I was being sucked and fucked at the same time, having both orgasmic feelings at once. I could have gone on forever with her beneath me in a sixty-nine and him behind me doggy-style.

A sixty-two-year-old woman wrote:

Many years ago my late husband and I were at a party. We had been drinking and eventually he stretched out on the sofa and fell asleep.

Finally, there were only four of us left, another couple and me, with my hubby still sacked out. The three of us enjoyed soft music and wine. I was dancing slowly with the husband and I felt his hard cock against me. I was a little worried about the wife seeing but I found out soon enough that I needn't concern myself. She got up and took my place and I could see he was doing the same thing to her. As they danced he pulled up her skirt at the back and I could see that she was not wearing panties.

I saw them look at me and smile, then he unzipped the back of her dress and she allowed it to slip to the floor. She was not wearing a bra either. I glanced at my husband but he was still out cold and snoring. The husband put his hand between his wife's legs while she freed his cock from his trousers and brought him to me. I did not think, I just took that lovely cock into my mouth.

Taking my hand, she urged me to their bedroom and helped me off with my dress, bra, and panties. I needed no foreplay. He sat on the end of the bed and she placed a small mirror on a stand on the floor. Then she told me to straddle her husband.

Oh, God. I looked into the mirror as I sucked his cock and it was one of the sexiest things I have ever seen. Eventually we fucked as I watched in the mirror while his wife sat beside me, masturbating. After I came we changed places and I watched him fuck her the same way. My husband never found out.

A sixty-eight-year-old man wrote:

One evening my wife told me that some time previously a male friend of ours had made erotic suggestions to her, telling her that he "wanted her." I was a bit surprised when she said that she hadn't immediately rebuffed him. She maintained that it was because she was well liquored up at the time but I sensed that there was more to it than that. I was aware she was checking my reaction and, in essence, asking for my approval. I told her she should go ahead and do it.

She looked at me and said, "If I went and screwed John [not his real name] you wouldn't mind?"

I answered that as long as she had no objections to me getting it on with John's wife, and she related all the dirty details after she did it, it would be okay with me! She pretended she wasn't convinced, but a while later I brought up the subject and encouraged her to go for it. She said that now she was reluctant because she assumed that the only reason I was agreeing was that I was trying to bed John's wife. I admitted I had that in mind but as long as she was doing it, I didn't see how she could lay restrictions on me.

One night some weeks later, when we were all well and truly shitfaced, they headed off together. Sadly I got a raw deal because John's wife wouldn't let me get close to her. I never did get it on with her.

When we got home later that night my wife refused to relate the details, as we had agreed. When I asked her how it had been she simply said, "It was too rushed. He came too quickly."

We went to bed and hell, did we ever have good sex. We did it five or six times in the ensuing twenty-four hours. Maybe it was the excitement of knowing what she had done, but considering that we had been married over twenty years at that time five times in a day is quite something.

A *thirty-five-year-old bisexual woman wrote:*

One evening not too long ago my husband and I were visiting another couple, longtime friends of ours. We started playing around and one thing led to another. Soon we were all having oral with our spouses. Then the two ladies started playing around a little while the hubbies watched. After the ladies were too hot to handle any more waiting the other lady grabbed my husband and I grabbed hers and we all had sex in the same room and same bed. We liked the experience so well that now we do it at least once a month. The last time we had three couples instead of just two.

HAVE YOU EVER DREAMED ABOUT WATCHING OR BEING WATCHED?

Making love in public is a common fantasy that some people have actually acted out. Ed and I made love several times on a balcony outside the bedroom of a large house we stayed in. The porch faced the side of the house, but anyone looking up the driveway could have seen us. Although no one ever did, the thought that someone might added spice to the lovemaking. Of the respondents to my survey, 85% of the men and 61% of the women fantasized about watching or being watched; 65% of the men and 67% of the women dreamed about making love in public.

Let's see what your neighbors are dreaming about.

A *twenty-one-year-old woman* wrote:

> I do think about it, but I've never done it. The thought of knowing someone could be watching is a turn-on but I would not want someone sitting right there in front of me. Maybe *peeping* would be a better word for it. And of course, they would see what a great lover I am.
>
> Watching another couple would definitely be a turn-on, too, but I think I would get so hot that I would have to join in.

A *twenty-six-year-old woman wrote*:

Sometimes I imagine what it would be like to have someone watch us making love, and the idea excites me tremendously. I would never try to act it out, though.

A *thirty-eight-year-old woman wrote*:

I love to fantasize about being in a hotel much like one I visited in Las Vegas. It's a square, built around a central courtyard. All the inner walls are glass, and there are no curtains.

Everyone gets to watch everyone else have sex like watching live porno. My boyfriend and I have sex, too, and everyone stops to watch us. And being a fantasy, I have a fantastic body.

A *thirty-nine-year-old bisexual woman wrote*:

Sometimes I dream that I'm the center of attention at a party, the only one not wearing clothes. My mistress is a tall, statuesque, beautiful blonde. She has me blindfolded, my hands are tied above my head, my feet spread and chained to eye hooks on the floor. Everyone at the party wants to see my pussy shaved so she orders another woman there to do it. In doing so, the woman caresses my pussy lips and clit, sticking her fingers into my vagina, making me moan. Throughout the evening, everyone has a chance to delight themselves and me on orders of my mistress, culminating in many orgasms.

A *thirty-year-old man wrote*:

A sexy, faceless woman and I are somewhat drunk while getting ready to leave a party. We decide to fuck in the limo on the long drive back to the hotel so to prepare, she goes into the ladies' room and removes her bra and thong panties. I go into the washroom and take off my underwear.

When we get in the limo there is already another couple in it, an attractive pair in their early fifties. After some small talk the other couple say they don't mind so we decide to do it anyway. I kiss her for a bit, then remove her top and suck her nipples while the couple watch. She straddles me as I lift her skirt and show our guests her moist cunt and asshole. The watchers sit silent, with seemingly only mild interest.

I push my partner back into her seat and pull off her dress, displaying her to the other couple. I begin to lick her clit and finger her cunt while the other two slowly become visibly hot and aroused. I reach for a champagne bottle and begin to fuck her with it, then I drink from it. I pour some on her asshole and lick and finger her there as she fucks her pussy with her finger.

She sucks my cock for a bit and then she straddles me again, facing the others, showing them her cunt as she spreads her lips to take my cock. By this time they are touching themselves and each other, but as aroused as they become, they are unable to keep from watching us. My partner becomes quite verbal at this point, talking about how great it is to have a cock inside her. I may fuck her ass also, but in any case I pull my cock out and spray the cum all over her cunt lips and pubic hair so our ride mates can see.

When we are exhausted, we watch them as they do it. They are really shy about it, having never performed in public before, but we have made them so hot that they can't help themselves.

A fifty-nine-year-old man wrote:

Although I've never actually done it, I think I would enjoy watching and being watched. I have mentioned it to my wife and she seems to think that, if we were out walking and came upon another couple making love in a clearing, watching silently from a discreet distance would be okay. I would prefer to meet another couple (no one I know, because no one I know would do this) for the theater, then we could come back to our house or go to theirs to have drinks and fun conversation. Soon, after some erotic talk, each couple would start making love.

As we all lie in front of the fireplace (I like a fireplace), we would stop and watch the other couple. He would slowly remove her blouse and bra and once she was topless, he would pay lots of attention to her nipples and neck. He would move down to remove her panties and spend lots of time eating her. She would remove his clothes and suck him and then they would sixty-nine for a while. Occasionally one or the other of them would look over at my wife and me and smile.

While we watch, she would put a condom on him with lots of lubricant, then instruct him to enter her ass. After a while he would remove the condom and she would suck him off. She would only swallow part of his load and allow part of it to run down her chin. He would lick off the remains and then it would be our turn. My wife and I would put on quite a show.

A *fifty-eight-year-old woman wrote:*

Since we enjoy making love outdoors, and in some pretty public places, it's not inconceivable that my husband and I have had an audience at one time. I'd prefer it were accidental so I wouldn't know that we were being observed until the passion had reached the point of no return. Then I wouldn't be self-conscious.

A *twenty-seven-year-old man wrote:*

I would love to be watched by other couples. My scenario is that perhaps we are on a stage, making love, kissing, hugging, sliding in and out, giving a tutorial to several nude couples who were near enough to touch.

A *thirty-year-old man wrote:*

I would love a large group to watch me spray my come into a woman's mouth or lick her cunt. I would want them to pleasure themselves during the act, and I would love to watch other couples fuck.

Preferably I would get to jerk off onto a woman's face or breasts while she is being fucked. It would also be nice to go for double penetration.

A *forty-year-old man* wrote:

In my fantasies I would either have an audience in the room or have someone watching a tape of my wife and me.

In real life, however, I'm sure as hell not going to have a tape made of us and I would never risk alienating anyone I know over a sexual fantasy. I wouldn't risk the possible complications of involving a stranger in our sex life, either.

A *forty-five-year-old man* wrote:

I have thought about videotaping my girlfriend and me but that can be somewhat risky. I think I mentioned the possibility at one time but it didn't get an enthusiastic response.

I would like to watch another couple, who didn't know my lady and I were watching, go at it. Well, not exactly watching in the "live" sense, I guess. I would love to hear a couple making love in the hotel room next door while we did likewise.

A *forty-eight-year-old man* wrote:

I used to work in a supermarket bagging groceries, and there were two good-looking lesbians who shopped there. I didn't think about sex with them, but I did fantasize about watching them make love with each other. I could get an erection just fantasizing about that.

A *fifty-year-old man* wrote:

I am definitely a very voyeuristic person but have never watched or been watched.

The closest we've come to doing it in public was last spring on a long weekend getaway to the Dominican Republic. After a night out clubbing and partying we were out on the balcony of our room and proceeded to get it on. Both of us stripped down and my wife began to suck my cock. It was quite late at night and nobody whom we knew of was watching us, but it was pretty risqué by our standards.

As far as my watching, I think the scene from *Blue Velvet* where the character hides in the closet while Dennis Hopper's weird character does his thing with Isabella Rossellini is the best. The thought of watching something unfold while I'm hidden away is very titillating.

A fifty-five-year-old man wrote:

Long ago we had neighbors who were none too careful about closing their drapes. One night my wife and I watched them, then had one of the most passionate nights of lovemaking in our entire marriage.

A sixty-two-year-old man wrote:

The first time I ever watched a couple actually making love was in a sex club in Sweden back in the 1960s. Good fun. Several times since, I've watched a couple privately. The husband would eat her out while I looked on, then she would give me a blow job while he watched. It turned all of us on but they did not want to "three" it. Each act was individual. She and I screwed several times alone when he was away on business trips.

A forty-year-old man wrote:

I've fantasized about my wife wearing a short skirt with no panties underneath and "unwittingly" exposing herself to men of various ages. I'm not sure how to do this without her being arrested.

A twenty-one-year-old woman wrote:

I think about making love in public all the time. I love the thought of being caught or knowing that someone could be watching me, but I don't want to know that they are there. It is a pure adrenaline rush when I'm having sex knowing there is a possibility of getting caught.

A fifty-one-year-old man wrote:

I've fantasized about masturbating in front of a group of people, in a contest perhaps, about who could squirt the farthest.

Others have made love where someone else might see, or have actually watched others.

A forty-five-year-old woman wrote:

I think the very best sex my husband and I ever had was on a beach in the early 1980s. We had been sunning ourselves on a public beach on the Gulf side of Florida. I was lying faceup, and he was lying facedown to hide his erection. We had been kissing for what must have been hours and he was up on his elbows and his mouth was over mine. Those kisses were incredible. He used his tongue to sketch the outlines of my lips and I did the same to him. He stuck out his tongue and as though it was his penis, I "fellated" it. We sucked each other's tongues, and rubbed our swollen lips against each other.

We talked dirty to each other, too, whispering wonderful things like, "I wish your cock was in me right now, pushing me down into the sand." I remember that he tortured me with his words, telling me how he wanted to bury his face in my wet pussy, how he wanted to lick my juices until my thighs were raw from his closely shaved face, how much he wanted to spread my ass cheeks and pound into me, right there on the beach. We didn't, of course, as it was daylight and there were families and people all around us.

Finally, when our passion was provoked almost to the maximum, I said, "Let's find a quiet place." Since our car was parked in a public parking lot, that wasn't an option, so we picked up our blanket and started looking in the Florida scrub for a little open space among the palms and pines.

We came upon a sandy spot about ten feet square back in the scrub, just on the edge of the Intracoastal Waterway. As Dan spread our blanket, we looked all around, even glancing across the waterway. No people, nothing except a boat ramp that looked unused.

Dan sat down, and I lay against him between his legs. I could feel his delicious erection between my shoulder blades. He cupped my breasts and began to kiss my neck, then pulled the straps of my swimsuit down. For the first time in my life my breasts were exposed to the sunshine. It felt wonderful when I clasped his hands as they squeezed my breasts.

Soon his hands began to move south toward my very soggy pussy. As his fingers slipped under my one-piece suit to probe beneath, I got impatient and pushed the suit down and kicked it off. There I was naked, still lying against him, his cock hard, held tightly by his tiny Speedo. I knew his cock's tip was bulging out over the waistband since I had been watching it wink at me all afternoon.

His fingers slipped into my wet crotch and found my erect clitoris. I moaned and felt as though my cunt and clit had been wanting his touch all afternoon. He continued to rub me with one hand while the other was on my breast. I was touching the hand in my cunt with my own fingers, urging him to go deeper.

When I came, it was an incredible wave of delight, freedom, sensuality, and desire. My body went rigid and convulsed, and he was whispering, "Oh, God, you are so beautiful. You look so hot. C'mon, baby, let it go." His fingers continued to dip into me then touch my ultrasensitive clit. I seemed to come for minutes.

He moved from behind me and pressed his face into my pussy. He licked for a while, then stood up and took off his swimsuit. His erection was enormous. Dan is extraordinarily endowed and his wonderfully curved cock, when erect, extends to just slightly above his navel.

He stood over me, touching his cock, and I remember him saying something like, "Okay, it's my turn. What should I do with this?" I could have opted to eat him until he came in my mouth or spread my legs there and invited him in, missionary-style, but I wanted it the way we enjoyed it the most: doggy-style.

I moved onto all fours, turning my ass to the waterway and letting my head fall onto my arms. He knew that this position meant one thing: hard fucking. That's the way we like it, especially after he has fingered me to orgasm.

He knelt behind me, held his cock against my wet labia, and I felt him lubricating it by moving it through my juices. Within seconds he was saying, "All right now, take it, sweetheart. Let me fuck you." I could feel his rod slide in, quickly and fully until it was as deep as it could go. Then he stopped and held completely still. We both love it when he makes us both wait. I remember hearing the water lapping, his breath in my ear, my own heart beating.

I felt his hands beneath me, cupping my breasts lightly. He tweaked my nipples, kissed my back, and listened to me saying, "Oh, Dan, give it to me. Come on, fuck me. Fuck me!" He remained still, circling my nipples with his fingers, pinching them as they sent erotic messages to my clit.

God, I wanted to feel him slamming into my ass, so that my tits would swing, and I could feel his balls slapping against my skin. I didn't want to kneel there on the sand with my butt in the air. I wanted to be *fucked!* "Fuck me, baby. Come on, Dan, fuck me, please. Please."

Then he started. He pulled his dick out of me slowly, verrrry slowly. When I felt the head pop out I was so let down because I thought that he had seen someone and our cover had been blown. "Dan!" I said.

Wham! His cock rammed into me. His fingers were on my clitoris, and I was facedown in the sand, nearly eating the grains. I had my mouth open, encouraging him by moaning and saying, "Fuck me, fuck me," over and over. My breasts were swinging and bumping with each thrust, which really turned me on. He was saying to me, "You want it! You want it! You want my cock in you hard and fast!" I could answer only with grunts.

We pumped for a long while until we were both breathless and soon I felt that familiar stiffening against my ass; his pumping and thrusting was giving way to the preorgasmic rigidity of his hips. Soon I heard him grunt in the way he always did, crying out, "Oh God, oh God!" I felt the spurts of semen as his hips thrust and drove his cock into me over and over. Soon there was semen flowing from my cunt, mixing with my juices, covering my greedy fingertips.

He collapsed on top of me, grinding me into the sand. What a wonderful feeling it was, hearing his labored breathing and feeling his cock soften inside me. He kissed my back, pulled his cock out, and fell over next to me on the sand. I rolled down and sucked the last of the juices off him, then licked my lips.

Then we heard applause. *Applause???* We couldn't imagine where it was coming from. We looked around and there, across the waterway, were three men at the water's edge, leaning against an SUV with a boat attached. They had been watching us for who knows how long, and they were applauding the show they had watched. I felt like standing up and bowing. Instead, I just kissed Dan one more time to thank him for making love to me.

A *seventy-eight-year-old man* wrote:

The best sex I ever had was on a beach in Christchurch, England, when we knew we were being observed by a group of teenagers from a little hill above. It was the exhibitionism that added spice.

A *twenty-three-year-old man* wrote:

I've done it in a grocery store. You can't get much more public than that.

A *fifty-eight-year-old woman* wrote:

We enjoy playing in public places because it's a turn-on, not for the sake of being seen. I like to pull over and make love on a secluded side road or a deserted beach or even in the backyard. There's a pond near our house and we've made love there, knowing others are around not really grasping what we're doing.

A *thirty-two-year-old man* wrote:

We have had sex in public, and the risk of being caught is very exciting. We both enjoy teasing each other so that our arousal is very apparent to bystanders. My wife loves to tease me in a shopping mall so that I have to walk around with a hard-on. I, in turn, enjoy it when she wears revealing clothes so I can caress her in front of other people. She gets embarrassed when her nipples poke out for all to see. We usually attack each other in the car before we get home.

A sixty-eight-year-old man wrote:

The closest thing to public sex that I have had was being totally naked in the backseat of our car, fucking like sex was going out of style. It was after dark and I really don't think anyone could have seen us unless they had been peeping. Nevertheless, the thought of it still turns me on!

A seventy-seven-year-old man wrote:

Actually we finally made my partner's fantasy come true when we had sex at the local beach. It was very exciting for both of us.

A sixty-year-old man wrote:

Several years ago my wife and I did it outdoors while on vacation in Denmark. We were lying on a blanket on a lawn at eleven-thirty at night just three meters from three couples who were standing on the far side of a hedge. The couples stood on the road for quite a while, talking to each other, not knowing we were fucking our hearts out just ten feet away. There was a lamp-post, and, if they had known, they could have seen us!

A forty-seven-year-old man wrote:

I love sex in unusual places and get super hot thinking others are watching. My wife likes more privacy so it probably won't happen.

I was watched a couple of times getting blow jobs in the car from other women before I was married. Once after lunch at work years ago I was with a secretary whom I was seeing who would not have intercourse with me but who would blow me as often as I'd like (yup, a guy's dream girl!!!!). We would have a very quick lunch and, since we only had an hour or so, drive to an empty parking lot or a secluded spot on a dirt road. Once we parked beside what we thought was a parked truck, but, while it was parked, it was not empty. The trucker had been sleeping. When he woke up he actually watched me getting head.

A *twenty-six-year-old bisexual woman wrote:*

Several years ago I watched my then-girlfriend have sex with her male lover. It was a weird experience but in the end I was okay with it.

I've been watched, too. Last time we had a threesome my boyfriend discreetly fucked me while I was kissing and stroking a female friend. She didn't comment, so I don't know what was going through her head—it didn't feel like a particularly voyeuristic setup.

In my voyeuristic fantasies I would be asked to counsel lovers who are having relationship difficulties about how to enhance their sensual lives. I would sit in a chair and direct them as to exactly what to do. They would follow my directives faithfully, and begin to have the type of sexual fulfillment they only dreamed of.

A *forty-seven-year-old woman wrote:*

Recently I was at a party and people were drinking a lot. One guy got really drunk so my boyfriend volunteered to drive him home in his car while someone else followed to drive my boyfriend back to me. It took quite a while so eventually I was one of the few people left.

I was bored sitting in a chair, flipping through a magazine, waiting for my ride. A couple whom I didn't know settled on a sofa and started kissing. Eventually they started the touchy-feely stuff. Her head was in his lap and I heard the sound of a zipper. I pretended to keep reading but, as you can imagine, I was really concentrating on the couple necking.

Soon she was in her underwear and his shirt was off. She was stretched out on her back while he dived between her legs. I was both embarrassed and excited so I couldn't resist finding a phone and calling my boyfriend on his cell phone. I told him what was going on and asked him to come back as soon as he could.

By the time I returned to the living room the guy's pants were off and he was fucking the girl while she told him to push harder. They ended up on all fours on the couch with the guy behind. They came, noisily, obviously oblivious to me.

While I digested that, I heard him ask whether she wanted it in the ass. That was enough for me. I got my coat and walked downstairs. Oh, and on the way home, my boyfriend and I did it in the car.

A *seventy-seven-year-old man* wrote:

My wife and I were in the swimming pool making out when we suddenly discovered that two kids had climbed our mango tree and were watching us. I yelled at them and one nearly fell trying to get down as quickly as he could. We were laughing so hard we never did finish and that spoiled it for us.

We have watched another couple having sex as well. It happened quite by accident when we "caught" my neighbor, a middle-aged widow, and her boyfriend. They were in her backyard when they thought I was away. My wife and I watched the whole thing and got so "hot" that we were playing with each other right there in the yard. It was almost like watching a porno movie. We've spent time with them on several occasions since and all I can see when I look at them is him going down on her. We've never told them we watched.

A *forty-seven-year-old man* wrote:

My girlfriend lives on a hill in San Francisco, and her small kitchen window overlooks the next house, which is several feet below hers. We got home last Friday about midnight and I walked over to the sink to pour out the remains of a soda that had gone flat.

Standing over the sink with the light out, I glanced down and saw a couple on a bed, in clear view, kissing. The light by the bed was on and her top was completely off. The guy was playing with her breasts and sucking on her nipples. They looked like they had just gotten home after a night out because he still had a white dress shirt and tie on, and she wore only dress slacks. I motioned my girl over and showed her the scene. She became as enthralled as I was.

After kissing and breast play, we watched as they undressed and kissed again while he rubbed her breasts and she stroked his penis. He then lay on his back, and we could see his erect penis sticking straight up as she leaned over him and took it in her mouth. Her head bobbed as she slowly stroked the shaft of the penis with her hand as she sucked and kissed it.

We could not believe what we were watching but it was really hot for us. After he got some oral stimulation, he got between her legs and began doing the same to her. Her knees were up with her back arched and she held his head as he licked away. After a few minutes he inserted his penis and the thrusting began. He was up on his arms looking down, and her legs were up and bent at the knees. As he thrust, her legs bucked.

They shifted position until she was on all fours, so he could drive his penis into her doggy-style. The thrusting began again and her breasts swayed as his penis pounded into her. He must have come while we watched because he did some hard slow pushes, then reached around and squeezed her breasts.

Eventually she got up and left the room, then came back with a towel to clean them both. We could see them on their backs now, and I could see her pubic hair, the dots of her nipples, and his limp penis as she caressed it.

It was amazing that this was all happening about ten feet away from our viewing area. I need to say that we would never look in people's windows or anything deliberately. This just happened by accident. I'm not sure they realized that they could be seen, but we had a great time watching, and more fun afterward. Boy did it make us hot.

DO YOU FANTASIZE ABOUT BEING IN CONTROL OR GIVING UP CONTROL DURING SEX?

Have you ever fantasized that you were in total control of a sexual encounter? Maybe you are a pirate ravishing a captive, or possibly a policeman having your way with a criminal. Or, on the opposite side, have you ever thought about giving up complete control of an encounter? Maybe you are the captive or the criminal, forced to submit to the desires of your captor. Or maybe it goes farther into the realm of delicious fantasy rape.

Is there anything wrong with that type of fantasy? Not at all. No one should confuse a fantasy that excites during sex or masturbation with a desire to act it out. Sexual fantasies are normal, and most of us have them in one form or another.

Of the respondents to my survey, 78% of the men and 87% of the women would love to either be in control of or be controlled by their partner during sex.

As with other fantasies, some dream, others actually act out their dreams.

A twenty-two-year-old woman wrote:

I have discovered I am a submissive. I have yet to pursue that avenue of myself much, but control is a big part of that.

A twenty-three-year-old woman wrote:

It is a totally thrilling thought to be powerless, at the mercy of someone else.

A twenty-five-year-old woman wrote:

I want him to be in total control and use chains or whips or restrain me in a swing while I'm tied up and blindfolded.

A thirty-one-year-old woman wrote:

I would love it if I could give up complete control, but I know he'd never play along with it.

You might be surprised. Try stretching your arms over your head and gently saying, "What are you going to do to me?" It might trigger something wonderful.

A thirty-five-year-old woman wrote:

Oh, yes, I'd love to try. I think I'd enjoy extreme bondage: all four limbs tied to the bed, being blindfolded, taking orders. It gets me hot just thinking about it.

A thirty-eight-year-old man wrote:

Yes, but I have never acted it out. I like to be controlled. I like to have someone take charge and tell me what to do. I'd even like to be taken by a man. I fantasize about being dominated.

A forty-one-year-old woman wrote:

Bondage and submission are my most frequent fantasies. We have tried it with me tied to the bed or my hands bound together, and when I am in the right mood, it's very exciting.

A forty-seven-year-old woman wrote:

I've tried some mild bondage with my husband. I wouldn't trust too many people.

Trust is a very basic part of any control game. If you can't trust your partner to stop when you ask or to say "stop" when it gets unpleasant, don't play.

A thirty-six-year-old man wrote:

I would love to be tied down or tie my wife down. I'd love to tease the hell out of her with toys while she was blindfolded or be teased myself.

A forty-year-old man wrote:

I usually fantasize about being controlled. I'd have her tie me up or tell me what to do. My wife has tied me up on occasion. Although it's always my idea, I think she likes it, too. After a while she gets impatient and wants to be stuck with my poker, which is kind of hard to do unless the man is in charge.

Not really. She could say, "Stick it in me, and you'd better make it good or else."

A forty-seven-year-old man wrote:

God, I'd love it. I dream about her not letting me come and teasing me until I can barely stand it any longer. I don't think she'd go along with it, however.

A fifty-year-old man wrote:

My wife tied me up and pleasured me once. It took a while for me to coax her to try it but once she did, it was great. Much as I'd love to do the same to her, she'll have none of it. The loss of ultimate control is not up her alley.

A fifty-six-year-old man wrote:

I think being tied up and played with over a long period of time, including oral and anal penetration, without being allowed to come would be wonderful. I would also like to do that to her!!!!

A thirty-nine-year-old bisexual woman wrote:

The idea of being controlled makes me hot and sexually hungry.

I want to be told what to wear, told to put a cucumber in my pussy in a restaurant, or ordered to wear a sheer blouse, no bra, short skirt, or tight pants. I love to think about being dressed with no underwear or wearing crotchless panties, or even going out in public wearing a collar with D-rings on it. My master or mistress would continually tease and caress me in public, making me be quiet while he or she probed my body, bringing me to orgasm.

A *thirty-five-year-old woman* wrote:

I would love for a cop to pull me over for a traffic violation, then tell me to follow him. He would take me to an alley and force his authority on me, if you get my drift.

A *thirty-one-year-old woman* wrote:

One of my favorite fantasies is that I'm a sexual guinea pig. I am in a glass room, suspended by something hanging from the ceiling, with my elbows and knees resting lightly on a doctor's table below me. Men in white coats are outside the room, watching me through a window as one of them manipulates long tools through a box in the wall. He arbitrarily inserts and withdraws a variety of instruments into both my pussy and ass. Little pads with wires are connected to my clit, my nipples, and my face, measuring my reaction to the stimuli. The man gets rather carried away and eventually brings me to a shuddering orgasm as his coworkers come in their pants at his side.

A *thirty-one-year-old woman* wrote:

I like to fantasize about having a "boy-toy" (a grown submissive man) who lives at our house just to serve me, whenever my husband is busy or too tired. When my husband is not too busy he is incorporated into our play in a very subservient role.

I like making my toy do things that he wouldn't do on his own, like suck my husband's cock, or bend over and spread his cheeks for an "inspection" while my husband watches and laughs. He always prepares my body for my husband's use by licking me completely clean . . . every inch . . . and I cannot possibly be considered clean if I haven't come at least once. Then, if he's good, he may play with himself while he watches us fuck. If he's been really, really good, my husband might let him fuck my ass while I'm sucking my husband's cock.

A *thirty-four-year-old woman wrote:*

I am confined in a specially made box that keeps me on my knees with my chest against the box's cold, wooden floor. My breasts hang down through two large holes and my ass and cunt are pushed against an opening behind me. I can't see anything while my box and I are sent out on the street. All sorts of men come up and play with my nipples and fuck me all the time . . . and I can't see them at all.

A *fifty-one-year-old woman wrote:*

I've fantasized about being "made" to have sex with my husband exactly the way he wants it. I dream about being totally controlled by him, having him tell me everything to do, and smacking me if I don't perform correctly. It probably sounds strange, but it really turns me on sometimes. I've never told him because I think he'd find it weird.

A *twenty-seven-year-old man wrote:*

I fantasize about being turned into a female, dressed in silky underwear, a filmy blouse, and a tight skirt. I'm given breasts, I don't know how, and raped by strap-on–wearing women over and over. I'm turned into a slut, used over and over until I am sore, whimpering. I would like to act out a less painful version of it.

A *thirty-three-year-old man wrote:*

I fantasize that my wife locks me in a chastity belt for an entire year. During that year she teases and arouses me to an impossible level of sexual excitement and frustration while never allowing me release. At times during the year, she restrains me and removes the chastity belt. During this time she teases me, strokes and sucks me, massages me, constantly promising me that I will finally be given that ever-precious orgasm. Then she will deny me and lock me back in the chastity belt. I would *love* to act this fantasy out.

A forty-seven-year-old man wrote:

One of my favorites is a rape fantasy, one that I played out with a girlfriend several years ago. Let me make this clear—she was willing. Very willing. She and I had kidded about it in our sexual games, and we decided to make it happen.

To act out the fantasy she left her back door open, and was watching TV. I "snuck" in, slipped behind her, and gagged her. She struggled, but not enough to alert the neighbors or anything. I had a toy water pistol, which I used to subdue her. I did her on the floor, with her trying to get away all the time, then spanked her and took her upstairs. There I threatened her and made her blow me. When she bit my dick lightly, I spanked her some more, then I left her tied up and went outside.

After about an hour I returned, used my key to get in, and "found" her still struggling to untie herself. We made mad, passionate love. It was great.

A fifty-eight-year-old woman wrote:

I love to think about being totally controlled by my partner, yet knowing that it is a completely safe situation. One of the fantasies I love involves a "pleasure chamber" where my lover blindfolds me, cuffs my hands together, and attaches me to a hook in the ceiling, leaving my body totally available to him to play with. I told my long-distance boyfriend about it once, then thought no more about it.

Much to my surprise, on one of my trips out to see him, my boyfriend made it come true. He has a room that used to be his daughter's dance studio and is now seldom used. The walls are mirrored. Well, when I arrived I found that he had installed this hook in the ceiling with a large cushioned stool under it and silk scarves to restrain me with. It was really exciting. He suspended me and tantalized me with all manner of wonderful things from vibrators to feathers before releasing me so we could make love on the sofa. What an incredible experience that was!

A sixty-two-year-old man wrote:

For me: The idea of soft bondage—where I cannot move and she works my body to bring me up and down until I am absolutely begging for climax—makes me crazy. My partner doesn't like to tie me down, so we pretend and I keep still as long as I can while she loves me. After a time I "have" to move. Being truly unable to move would be more intense.

For her: Sometimes she likes me to hold her down and pin her hands back while I am on top or hold them at her side while I lick her. She says it makes her feel wanted. My fantasy is to tie her down, first on her back, then on her stomach, and give her pleasure until she passes out. Or—tie her to a sex swing and do the same.

Here are a few letters from writers who have brought elements of control into their love life.

A forty-five-year-old man wrote:

Complete trust makes complete submission possible. We have done what some might consider fairly mild bondage—blindfolding, icing nipples (but never hot waxing). We've learned over the years that so much of the idea of control is tied to the place your head is, and to make that even better we carefully choose our tone of voice and language.

A twenty-seven-year-old woman wrote:

I have both controlled and been in control. I found that I don't like being controlled nearly as well. I love being in control of a "sub," someone I barely know.

A fifty-two-year-old man wrote:

We've played some domination games, complete with restraints (soft rope, scarves, handcuffs). Usually my wife is dominant. It's only an occasional game with us.

A thirty-one-year-old woman wrote:

I remember one night I spent with a friend. It was understood that there was no romantic interest between us, but there sure was a ton of chemistry. He was more than a little kinky, and I was more than a little curious.

For eight hours I was tied up in more directions than I can possibly describe, while he entertained himself with an entire suitcase full of toys, ramming and jamming them in every orifice he could find. I lost count of how many times I came, but I know a whole lot of inhibitions went out the window that night as he taught me more about my body than I had ever imagined. I was also pleasantly amazed that he came four separate times. It was phenomenal, and all about fun and pleasure.

A sixty-nine-year-old man wrote:

Yes! Yes! I would love to try it with my wife. Before I was married I placed myself under the total control of a Mistress for a whole weekend.

Unforgettable!

A thirty-two-year-old man wrote:

The best sex I ever had was the first time my wife blindfolded me and tied me to the bed. I lay waiting in anticipation for something to happen. Nothing did for several agonizing minutes.

Then I heard her vibrator and her moans as she played with herself in front of my helpless body. She told me every detail of what she was doing and I was forced to just listen and imagine. This drove me wild, and I was harder than I have ever been before. It lasted for about ten minutes, but seemed like an eternity at the time.

When I heard her moan as she climaxed and felt the bed shake I almost came all over myself without any touching. She lightly touched me, and put her come-soaked fingers in my mouth. She then sucked me slowly and lovingly for a long, long time, not letting me come.

After she had me worked up into a frenzy, she used her hand and mouth on me at the same time, squeezing me tightly and going up and down very slowly. Right before I was ready to erupt, she slid her vibrator between my cheeks and rubbed it lightly across my anus, without penetrating. It was the first type of anal play that I had experienced, and I literally exploded, sending strong jets of semen everywhere. It was definitely the most powerful orgasm I had ever experienced.

HAVE YOU EVER FANTASIZED ABOUT PAIN AS PLEASURE?

A s with other fantasies, pain is something that is usually left in the imagination. Of those who responded to my survey, 30% of the women and 43% of the men wrote that they had fantasized (or acted out) "pain as pleasure." Most qualified their answers—only slight pain, meant not as torture, but as an enhancement to lovemaking. Some wanted to administer the pain, others wanted to receive it. A few were anxious to experience either one. Why? Who knows or cares? It's just something that arouses some people. Here's what some had to say.

A *twenty-one-year-old woman* wrote:

I do not want to experience something that is very painful. Slight pain that is meant for pleasure is fine, but nothing harming. I would never go for the whips or anything like that. I have never experienced pain other than the slight pain during my first sexual experience but I think it might be exciting.

A *fifty-one-year-old man* wrote:

Maybe I'd like a good spanking followed by hot, hot sex. I'd like to be administering the whip, not striking the skin, just making it snap close to my lover's ear.

When I was young, I went to a cottage with my girlfriend; her older brother was there with his friends. I saw a decorative whip hanging on the wall over a fieldstone fireplace. While everyone was in the kitchen getting food ready, I took it down. There I was, alone in the great room, wielding that whip. I hadn't noticed that every time it snapped, I moaned as if I was being struck. One of the brother's friends was watching me with this look in his eyes that I didn't understand at that time. Now I wish I had pursued it.

A twenty-six-year-old woman wrote:

I've never tried it but light slapping might be fun. I'd want to be the slappee, not the slapper. I guess I like being the center of attention.

A thirty-one-year-old man wrote:

I don't fantasize about pain as pleasure for myself, but I have done some role playing where I spanked a naughty "schoolgirl" for neglecting her homework. It was really erotic and exciting.

A fifty-eight-year-old woman wrote:

Not real pain, but I have fantasized about being spanked (not hard) with a hand (no paddles or anything like that) while making love, or building up to it. I think I'd like the "bad little girl" thing like *The Story of O,* being restrained and letting him have his way with me. Perhaps just the quick slap on the ass while taking me from the back would be a turn-on. I really have to think more about this one.

A twenty-two-year-old man wrote:

I would love to have candle wax dripped over me, have proper nipple clamps attached to my body, be gagged and bound and whipped. I love my nipples being twisted—so I expect I'll enjoy other tortures, too.

A *forty-two-year-old man wrote:*

I fantasize about pain during sex, especially on my nipples. I would love my wife to pinch them really hard or bite them before and during sex. I know it would get me erect, and produce explosive orgasms. She wouldn't break the skin, but there would be bruises for days.

One time she accidentally kneed me in the nuts. I almost threw up, it hurt so much, but afterward we had sex three times in a four-hour period.

A *thirty-nine-year-old bisexual woman wrote:*

My fantasy sex begins with my refusal to undress or dress as per the wishes and instructions of my master or mistress. He/she strips me of my clothing and chains me between two trees, giving him or her complete access to my whole body. My master/mistress then blindfolds me so that I cannot see when and how my punishment is coming. He/she kisses and caresses me only to then use a slapper on the underside of my breasts. He/she whips my thighs and buttocks, then alternates between caressing gestures and using the slapper. He/she attaches nipple clamps, pinches, and whips on me, making me beg for release.

A *sixty-two-year-old man wrote:*

About as close as we come on this one is that my wife likes to have her hair pulled firmly during foreplay and more harshly just before climax. A tweak on the nipples pleasures her, too, first a lick, a suck, and then a quick jolt, building up toward climax. Even a gentle bite on her labia or harsh quick suck on her clit is pleasurable at times. Gentle pulls on pussy hair, just to the point of discomfort, are also good for her. None of this is required every time, just when we're in the mood!

A *thirty-one-year-old man wrote:*

I like moderate pain—deep scratching, slapping, hair pulling, etc.

As for acting out a real pain scene I think the outfits are so silly that I can't see getting into B&D.

A forty-seven-year-old man wrote:

I have been tied up on a couple of occasions. The best happened years ago in Phoenix at a resort. My girlfriend and I were playing and she wanted to tie me up. I was game, so she placed me facedown on the bed, then tied my arms and legs—snugly, but not tight. Then she left the room!!!!

She had been gone for about half an hour when I heard the key in the door. It *wasn't* her. It was the maid, and she got an eyeful of my bare ass. I could swear I heard the whoosh of breath from her mouth in surprise. Seconds later my girlfriend came in and we both told the woman all was well, so she left. My girlfriend stood over the bed and acted ticked off at me for showing my ass to another woman. Slowly, making sure I knew exactly what she was going to do, she took the belt from my pants and began spanking me, hard. When she decided to make it a bit more personal, she spanked me with her hand.

I was getting immensely turned on, and she was well aware of it. She couldn't see my huge erection, of course, because I was facedown, but from my movements, bucking my hips so my cock rubbed against the bedspread with each smack, she knew it. The spanking continued, and I kept moving, rubbing against the satin. I ended up coming, spurting all over the covers.

It wasn't the end of it. She spanked me some more, then untied my hands and made me lick up some of my sperm. It was so degrading, yet so hot. I don't think anything like this could have happened with a casual lover, but we were very close and it worked out well.

She and I incorporated spanking into our lovemaking from that point on. It was me being spanked at first, generally over her knees. Later she agreed to be spanked and I warmed her bottom. She learned to enjoy it as much as I did.

A twenty-seven-year-old woman wrote:

Sometimes I like being spanked or having my nipples pinched or bitten a little. I haven't been really into a lot of pain, though.

My fantasy is a scenario in which I've been spanked or taken roughly. Kind of a mock-rape thing, where I don't have any say, and he spanks me and fucks me any way he wants. He also makes me pleasure and suck him.

A forty-three-year-old woman wrote:

We've played hard enough that my husband has put bruises on my ass because I kept on telling him harder, harder, and harder. I just love to have my ass spanked good and hard. I love being the bad girl who deserves to be spanked and fucked up the ass as only a bad girl deserves.

A twenty-seven-year-old man wrote:

We have bitten, choked, and scratched each other. She loves to twist my nipples until I scream in agony. It makes my cock harder and longer, too.

A forty-year-old man wrote:

I enjoy enough pain to be uncomfortable, but not excruciating. I like it when she bites my abdomen, pokes my navel, or squeezes my balls when she is excited. I like to hear her wince or whimper whenever I thrust my well-lubricated cock into her anus. Quickly her whimpers of pain turn to moans of pleasure.

A forty-eight-year-old man wrote:

My nipples are always the surest way to excite me, and I love having them played with—the rougher the better—before and during sex. Before sex it's the surest way to get me erect, and during sex it is the fastest way to bring me off. If she does it right I'll be tender for a week, which is fantastic.

A twenty-five-year-old man wrote:

I enjoy pain during sex. I love to be bitten on the neck hard enough to slightly break the skin. And I like my nipples to be bitten also—hard but not too hard. My wife and I have learned exactly what works best.

A forty-five-year-old man wrote:

My wife and I have played games like this enough that I introduced the concept of a safe word to her. We don't do control that often in a way that I think a safe word would be needed, but we are both more comfortable knowing it's there. I gave her an erotic spanking hard enough one time that I thought she might use a safe word but she didn't. She later described that as a memorable encounter. And it was great knowing that I could do what I wanted and that she would stop me if it got too bad.

She doesn't ask to be controlled or spanked, but when I take the initiative and dominate her, her responses tell me she gets pleasure from this. Interesting part is, she has never openly admitted this. One of my goals is to encourage her to discuss it.

A "safe word" is an uncommon word—say, *marshmallow*—that, when used by either player in a pain or control situation, means *stop now*, no questions asked. It frees both partners. The one who is controlling the situation, the dominant or top, can do whatever he or she wants, knowing the partner will use the safe word whenever things stop being pleasurable. The one who is controlled, the submissive or bottom, can scream, "No, don't!" knowing that nothing will stop unless the safe word is used. It's a wonderfully freeing feeling just submitting to the wishes of a partner.

As with everything else, it's wonderful for some and a turnoff for others. It's fabulous to have so many choices, isn't it?

HAVE YOU EVER HAD HOMOSEXUAL FANTASIES?

I asked folks to tell me whether, if they were straight, they'd ever had homosexual fantasies and, if gay, if they'd ever had straight ones. Of those who responded, 46% of the men and 33% of the women said, often in capital letters, that *No*, they hadn't had any such. Straight women were more apt to have homosexual fantasies, maybe because men find them so scary. Here's what some of your neighbors had to say.

A *twenty-one-year-old woman wrote:*

I am straight and I have thoughts about sex with my best girl-friend, but don't know that I would ever act upon that fantasy. I would like to see what it would be like to pleasure her and have her do the same to me. I'm really curious to know whether it is different—better—with a woman since, presumably, she knows pretty much what another woman wants.

A *forty-seven-year-old man wrote:*

I don't think I have homosexual tendencies, although I have a little secret, the one thing I never told anyone about. I engaged in a foursome once and I have mentioned to people how it was boy–girl. I will admit to you that the girls did convince us guys to give each other head. I licked his cock and he licked mine. I couldn't come, but he came in my mouth and I swallowed it. I was never so embarrassed, and later literally shook at the behavior. We never talked about it again.

A *thirty-two-year-old man wrote:*

I have had homosexual fantasies, but they always seem better as fantasies. So when I actually see guys naked, it does absolutely nothing for me.

A *thirty-six-year-old woman wrote:*

I wonder what it would be like to touch another woman's body—her breasts, her hair, her butt, her pussy. I also wonder what it would be like to have my face between her legs or sixty-nine with her. I wonder how different, if at all, receiving oral sex would be for a woman versus a man. Please understand that I can't imagine ever actually doing this.

A *nineteen-year-old woman wrote:*

I do dream about being with another woman, but I believe if I were ever to act it out it would ruin the fantasy. Besides, I am too old to be experimenting with stuff like that now. And of course it would require cheating on my husband, which I would never do.

A *twenty-two-year-old man wrote:*

I do have homosexual fantasies, although I don't think I could ever carry one out, partly because I've not met a man I fancied at all yet. My most vivid fantasy is being forced to have a man fuck my mouth.

A *sixty-year-old man wrote:*

No fantasies about being gay but I like to fantasize about watching homosexual women doing it to each other, especially performing oral sex. That must be a joy! So many juices for pleasure. If I were a woman, I think I would prefer to be homosexual!

A *fifty-nine-year-old straight man* wrote:

If I were the second male with a woman, I could put his member inside her with my hands if needed. Doing a double penetration would be on the agenda, too.

A *thirty-three-year-old woman* wrote:

I am straight but I have fantasized about being with another woman just to know what it would be like and to pleasure my partner who, I know, would want to watch.

A *fifty-one-year-old woman* wrote:

I would like to know how it feels to have a woman make love to me. I hear there is much gentleness and that it's very special.

A *twenty-six-year-old woman* wrote:

Yes, I do, and they've been increasing in frequency since moving to a city where bisexuality's more accepted. I think one of the reasons I fantasize so much is because I've never done it; who knows, maybe I'll kiss a woman and won't like it at all.

I think women's bodies are beautiful, in a different way from men's bodies—which I also love. I'm fascinated by the idea of touching a woman's breasts and belly, the softness of it as compared to the hardness of a man's body. I'm a little nervous about it, since it's an entirely new thing for me, and I haven't really had any opportunities to act out on it. I'm working on it, though. I think I'd want it to be someone I don't know well, but someone who's inherently sexy—someone who's attractive and just has sex appeal, male or female.

A *twenty-three-year-old woman* wrote:

A few times I've dreamed that someone was giving me oral sex and I open my eyes to find out it's a woman whom I don't know. My husband is watching from a chair across the room. I wake up really turned on.

A *twenty-five-year-old woman* wrote:

Several of my girlfriends and I were joking around with some guys at a party and told them we were going to so-and-so's hot tub to play with each other. All the guys went wild. I had a friend once who would have done something like that but I don't know where she is now. We used to dance together at parties and the guys would go crazy. We are both straight, but are also extremely open-minded and daring.

A *thirty-five-year-old woman* wrote:

I have had fantasies about being with another woman. It starts with passionate kissing and soft teasing rubs then moves on to oral sex play and fingering. We use vibrators and double dongs on each other. Finally I got so curious that I tried it. It was better than my fantasy. Yum!

A *forty-one-year-old woman* wrote:

Occasionally I fantasize about being forced to have sex with another woman while being watched by one or more men. In real life, however, I have no desire to experiment with another woman. I would probably be repelled by it.

A *twenty-seven-year-old man* wrote:

I have had homosexual fantasies. Mostly they involve a woman and a confirmed homosexual. The hot and lovely woman gently breaks down my defenses, getting me to let the guy touch me, then I touch him, he sucks me, I suck him, finally he takes my ass.

A *thirty-one-year-old man* wrote:

Homosexual fantasies accidentally slip into my psyche because I'm surrounded by attractive gay men in San Francisco. Frankly, however, I don't have any interest in gay sex. My own penis is worry enough.

A *fifty-year-old man* wrote:

An interesting question. I am definitely heterosexual, and have been my whole life. I've never experimented or anything re- motely like that. Lately, however, I must admit to being curious as to what it would be like to be "intimate" with another male.

My fantasy doesn't go anywhere near anal intercourse, giving or receiving, but it does definitely include rubbing, massaging, and penile pleasuring for both of us.

I guess I must grudgingly admit to being curious what it would be like to play with another's erect cock, and even sucking a guy off—and swallowing! It amazes me to admit that! Of late I have gone as far as to go on a couple of gay chat sites and put "feel- ers" out (no pun intended). There have been a couple of re- sponses, but I've not acted upon them, and I wonder whether I ever will. I guess I'm afraid of being caught in the act, or of the experimentation affecting my "normal" life afterward.

I've read that this type of homosexual curiosity is not unusual, but it still is a deep dark hidden secret desire. I've not even come close to sharing this thought with my wife or anyone else.

A *thirty-eight-year-old woman* wrote:

I have had lots of sexual dreams about making love with another woman, partly because I'm so curious and partly because I am al- ways so horny. I fantasize about what it would be like to touch a woman intimately, to go down on her, and to have her go down on me. Maybe part of the reason I wonder about it is that I don't have much experience being on the receiving end of great oral sex. It's something that I would like to know even if only once. Even though I am straight it drives me wild just thinking about it.

A *thirty-nine-year-old woman* wrote:

Here's one of my favorite fantasies. While vacationing in the tropical islands, I meet a beautiful self-assured woman. We frolic and play, caressing each other. The touch of her lips on my breasts and her fingers caressing my pussy lips drive me to ecstasy beyond belief. We explore each other, learning about ourselves and our partner's likes and dislikes. She learns that I like to be the submissive one so she uses that to her advantage by ordering me to kiss her lips, neck, breasts, thighs, and everywhere that pleases her. Then she does the same for me. We use a double-tipped dildo to fuck each other while rubbing breast to breast and French kissing. The vacation is one big long fuck fest.

A sixty-nine-year-old man wrote:

Phew. Well, here's my homosexual fantasy. While cross-dressed, I am fondled and taken roughly by a man I met in a gay bar.

A twenty-two-year-old man wrote:

My most vivid recent fantasy is being tied up while men and women use me as a sex object. I don't think I'd ever actually fancy a man in real life, but I often dream about being fucked by one. In my fantasy a man fucks my mouth, and another man takes me from behind while women suck my cock, twist my nipples. Then they all change places. Women sit on my face, blokes suck my cock—whatever goes, really, and I can't do anything to stop it.

seven

AND LASTLY...

The One Thing No One Knows about My Sex Life

THE ONE THING
I'VE NEVER TOLD
ANYONE ABOUT
MY SEX LIFE IS . . .

S ecrets. We've all got them—little ones and big ones. I was very curious to read what things my respondents had never told anyone. The most common answer was, "The number of lovers I've had." That's a fine secret. I don't think anyone needs to know how many people exist in a lover's past. Who cares whether you've been with one, a few, or the entire New York Giants football team? As long as you practiced safe sex and are in good health now, your previous relationships are none of anyone's business. All of your past has made you what you are today, and that's fine.

A *twenty-five-year-old woman* wrote:

Some people know some, but no one knows the complete number of men I've been with. The number is higher than I would like.

Also, I went to a strip club with my boyfriend last year. I wanted to get on stage so bad but I had to drive home that night and thus was unable to drink. No one knows how much I would have loved to have a couple of shots and climb on stage, then strip to nothing and dance. People think I'm only joking. They don't know I am serious.

Often, as I read the answers, I wondered why the respondent hasn't told his or her partner the secret. The saddest thing would be for two long-partnered people to have the same fantasy yet never find a way to share it. I made a few suggestions about sharing sexual secrets in the introduction of this book. If you've got something you'd like to share, look back and see whether you can make a few of your dreams come true.

A *twenty-three-year-old woman wrote:*

I wish I could be totally honest with my husband and not have him get insulted or annoyed. I would love for him just to get the urge to go down on me until I come, and not have any need for his own gratification.

A *twenty-seven-year-old woman wrote:*

No one knows that I really feel insecure about how I am as a lover.

A *thirty-one-year-old woman wrote:*

I feel like a complete nymphomaniac! I think about sex all the time, except when I'm at work. If I had the choice, I'd be having sex almost constantly. I would love to be a man's sex slave!

A *forty-three-year-old woman wrote:*

No one knows that I have a fantasy about my husband. In my fantasy my husband walks up to me while I'm sunbathing and forces me to have sex. He ties me to the lounge, spanks my ass until it's good and hot, fucks my ass, and comes all over my back. After he's done he releases me and lets me continue sunbathing.

A *forty-five-year-old woman wrote:*

I would like to have two men at a time, one in my cunt and one in my mouth pumping and thrusting. That's my secret fantasy.

A forty-seven-year-old woman wrote:

The only person I've ever told that I enjoy water sports is you.

A fifty-one-year-old divorced woman wrote:

No one knows that, although I was married for a long time, I have never had an orgasm. For a while I worked on it and tried to get my husband to do things to help me until I eventually realized it wasn't important to him. I never even had to fake it . . . he never seemed to notice and I never told him. I thought it wasn't important to me, either, but secretly I was mad as hell.

I've learned a lot since then and that guy and I are no more. I'm hoping to find someone who will understand and help me to learn about my body well enough to climax.

A fifty-eight-year-old woman involved in a long-distance relationship wrote:

Wow, tough question. Although my sex life is pretty tame, it's really important to me. I'm sometimes surprised by the many things that turn me on physically during the day, and how quickly I can reach orgasm without really trying. I wonder what this must say about me as a person.

I guess there isn't really anything I've never told anyone about my sex life, except how much I love sex, and how hard it is to live without it on a regular basis. As much as I enjoy my current relationship, having three thousand miles between us, and many, many, many weeks between visits, makes it very difficult to maintain a happy, healthy, sexual, and spiritual relationship.

A twenty-seven-year-old man wrote:

I've never told anyone about my desire to wear women's clothes. Actually I'd love to have a woman control me, maybe by threatening to tell my friends about this side of me. She would then shave all my body hair, dress me in a wig, bra, satin panties, a garter belt, stockings, high heels, and a woman's dress. Then she would force me to go out with her that way.

A *thirty-two-year-old bisexual man wrote:*

My bisexual thoughts are not the sort of thing I want known, although I would like to tell my wife someday.

A *forty-year-old man wrote:*

I've never told anyone just exactly how obsessed I am with sex. I think about having sex all the time. I dream about undressing women I meet during the day and eventually seeing them naked.

I am in no way dissatisfied with my wife's body or sexual technique; it's just that, although I'm able to satisfy my wonderment over her body, I can't do that with anyone else. I envy Europeans who live in a culture where topless females are the norm, and nude females aren't nearly as unusual as in America; Europe is way ahead of us in this regard.

When I look at a woman who catches my eye, I always wonder whether she notices, and if she does, how she feels about it. Does she like the admiration or resent the attention? Maybe she's baffled by the attention since she views herself as very ordinary. Maybe she wonders whether I'm thinking about more than just admiring the view.

A *forty-two-year-old man wrote:*

I've never told anyone, but if I could ever find someone like the lady I had a relationship with many years ago I'd never let her go. Sadly she was six years older than I was, and six years seemed insurmountable when I was in my early twenties.

This woman was the most fantastic sex partner I've ever been with, and probably one of the best anywhere. She truly enjoyed sex. She would "style" her bush, which was an incredible turn-on for me. In addition to shaving it, she would one time show up with it in curls, and another time bleached, and the next time dyed black (she was a natural redhead). She enjoyed doing it and I found it sexy as hell.

A forty-five-year-old man wrote:

No one knows that my wife and I both keep our genitals cleanly shaved because we agree that sex is much better and cleaner without the mess of pubic hair. We shave each other from time to time and usually end it with a test drive!

A forty-seven-year-old man wrote:

I've never told any of my partners about my passion for masturbation.

Why in the world not? Mutual masturbation can be a delicious part of lovemaking. Why not try inviting your lady to join you?

A forty-eight-year-old man wrote:

I wish I wasn't circumcised. My best friend growing up wasn't, and I envied his equipment. I've always liked to play with my penis, and I envied guys who had that bit more to play with than I had. That friend and I played with each other when we were growing up, as boys will do of course, and I really enjoyed sliding his foreskin up and back like it was something magical. If it were up to me, I'd like to have mine back. Not even my wife, partner, and best friend for twenty-six years knows that one.

A fifty-two-year-old man wrote:

Okay . . . I've told very few people this. Many years ago, although I was married, I had sex with one of my wife's former bosses. Let's call her Ann. I was in my early twenties and Ann was in her forties. Her husband had left her for his younger secretary and it had dealt a crushing blow to her self-image. She was starving for love and sexual activity and I was just in the right place at the right time.

She was a petite woman and, although she had no breasts at all, she had very prominent nipples and the largest vagina and labia I had ever seen. Our lust burned out of control and we enjoyed each other on two separate occasions. Although that was thirty years ago, I still think about it.

A seventy-seven-year-old man wrote:

When I first went through puberty, several of us had a "jack-off" club. We had contests to see who could come the fastest and shoot the farthest. While my partner knows about that part of it, I've never told anyone that I tried to fuck one of the kids in his rectum. I couldn't penetrate and that was the end of that but I've always worried that if I told anyone about it, they would think I was a "fairy," when it was just an early-teen experiment.

There is one other thing. When I was young I always thought that after-sixty sex was just a myth. How wrong I was! And how happy I am about it!

A seventy-eight-year-old man wrote:

What most people don't know? I never can have enough. It's the greatest.

Terrific. I think I'll make these wonderful men my poster children for sex after sixty, or seventy, or, soon, eighty.

A twenty-year-old woman wrote:

I never really told anyone that I would like to be with my best girl-friend. We have joked about it because our boyfriends over time have mentioned it as a fantasy of theirs, but I have never really told anyone that it's something I truly think about.

A twenty-six-year-old woman wrote:

I guess I've never told anyone how much better it gets as my partner and I are together more and more, longer and longer, partly because I never really thought about it until now. We have been together for almost fourteen years and I can't imagine feel-ing more loved, more comfortable, more in love than I am now. He's the only one I've ever been with and God willing, he will be the only lover in my life.

A *twenty-six-year-old woman* wrote:

I never told anyone how much I crave sex. The orgasms aren't as important as that wonderful feeling of being as close to my husband as I could possibly get, and I want to feel that several times a day. I love holding him inside my body and my arms. Since my pregnancy has been difficult, the doctors have ordered no sex until delivery (still three months away). I miss this feeling of "oneness" most of all.

A *forty-eight-year-old man* wrote:

I met someone on a plane about ten years ago. We hit it off, went directly to her hotel upon landing, and spent twelve hours doing everything we could think of. I've never done anything like that again, but I think of that day often.

A *twenty-two-year-old man* wrote:

There are two things I've never told: that sometimes I have homosexual fantasies, and that I'd love to perform for a group of women.

A *thirty-three-year-old woman* wrote:

I've never discussed with anyone that I'm turned on by anal play.

A *forty-seven-year-old woman* wrote:

Would you believe that I got paid once for it! My lips are sealed.

I'd love to hear more about that one!

A *forty-three-year-old man* wrote:

No one knows about my fetish for prolonged enforced abstinence via a chastity belt. I have divulged my interest in chastity belts to my wife, but I have never told her the extent to which I would like to carry this fantasy out.

A *fifty-year-old man* wrote:

I don't have a lot of chest hair, but I just can't tell my wife that I have a noticeable bit around my nipples. For quite some time I have clipped this hair, as I enjoy the semierotic feeling when the stubble catches on my T-shirt.

A *twenty-five-year-old woman* wrote:

I once had sex with three guys in the same day. I'm not ashamed of anything I've done sexually, but I don't want people to think I'm a nymphomaniac. I hate when I can't have sex whenever I want. My fiancé knows how much I love it and we usually do it two or three times a day.

A *thirty-year-old woman* wrote:

My sex life is great but if we do it too often, it ruins some of the fun for me.

A *sixty-two-year-old man* wrote:

After visiting a prostitute on a trip to the Far East, I got a minor kind of VD. I went to a public hospital there for a checkup, got pills, and it went away in about a week, just before I returned home to my partner at the time. I was sweating it out and I still feel a bit of guilt that I did something so dumb as not using protection.

A *thirty-five-year-old bisexual woman* wrote:

Other than me and hubby, no one knows that we have found swapping to be a total turn-on. During one swapping evening, I found that I am bisexual, but we keep that mostly to ourselves.

TO THE READER

Dear Reader,

As I organized the survey responses and incorporated them into this book, I was quite surprised at a few of the statistics and some of the answers. I found the sex lives of my neighbors fascinating and I think you did, too. You were probably also amazed at a few of the bits and pieces that you read here, and I hope you've added a few new ideas to your repetoire of sexual activities.

You'll find a slightly adapted survey at the back of this book so you can enjoy putting your own ideas onto paper. You can also download it at www.JoanELloyd.com/survey.txt. Obviously I can't change this book, but I might post some of the survey answers on my Web site or use them in another book. You might benefit by giving a copy of it to your partner, too, and later sharing your answers.

I'd love it if you'd visit my Web site, Joan Elizabeth Lloyd's Secrets for Lovers, at www.JoanELloyd.com. You'll learn a bit about me, read a new erotic story each month, and be able to swap ideas with other visitors in my Lovers' Feedback Forums. Drop me a note when you visit and tell me what you thought of *Naughty Secrets*.

If you want to send me questions, comments, or answers to my survey questions, I can be reached by e-mail at Joan@JoanELloyd.com, or by snail mail at Joan Lloyd, P.O. Box 221, Yorktown Heights, NY 10598. For snail mail, please allow four to six weeks for me to have time to answer. I look forward to hearing from you.

Joan

THE SURVEY

All material received in response to this survey will become the property of Joan Elizabeth Lloyd, without compensation, and may or may not be included in any future work. All responses will remain anonymous and will be edited as appropriate.

A TOTALLY UNSCIENTIFIC SURVEY OF SEXUALITY AND LOVEMAKING

There are only four pieces of information that I really need to tabulate the results:

Your age?_____ Your sex?_____ Gay or straight?_____
Are you permanently partnered right now? Y/N_____

Please answer some, or all, of the questions—those that interest you.

About You and Your Partner
1. Do you masturbate? How often? What makes it feel particularly good? Do you have a routine? Describe it for me.
2. Do you remember the first time you masturbated?
3. Do you need pornography, music, erotic stories to get you in the mood or does your imagination suffice?
4. Do you use any toys?

5. Does your partner know that you masturbate? How does he or she feel about it?

6. Does your partner masturbate?

Questions on Sex

1. What was the best sex you ever had? Tell me every juicy detail. What made it so great?

2. What was the worst sex you ever had? What made it so bad?

3. Do you think your best sex is yet to come?

4. Tell me about your first time.

5. Tell me about your most recent experience.

6. Have you told your partner how many lovers you've had?

7. What's the most embarrassing thing that ever happened to you while making love?

8. What's the most wonderful thing that ever happened to you while making love?

About Lovemaking with Your Partner

1. What do you wish your partner knew about making love with you?

2. What do you wish he or she would tell you?

3. Do you wonder whether you're a good lover? Have you ever asked?

4. Have you ever faked an orgasm?

5. Have you ever told someone he or she was great in bed when he or she really wasn't?

6. Do you usually make love with the lights on?

7. Do you usually make love at night?

8. Do you usually make love in the bedroom?

9. What is the most unusual place you've ever made love? Tell me all the delicious details.

10. What's the wildest thing you've ever done during sex?

11. Is there a sexual thing you've done that you now regret? What happened? Why do you regret it?

12. Do you have a favorite position for lovemaking? Describe it as best you can.

13. What is your partner's favorite position/activity? Do you like it, too, or do you do it to please him or her?

14. Do you and your lover engage in oral sex? If not, why not?

15. If yes, do you enjoy it, or do you just do it to please your partner?

16. Do you and your lover engage in anal sex? If not, why not?

17. If yes, do you enjoy it, or do you just do it to please your partner? Do you think your partner enjoys it or does it for you?

18. How often do you and your partner play with toys? Never? Sometimes? Always? Describe.

19. Why did you decide to bring toys into the relationship?

20. Where did you get the toys? Were you embarrassed?

21. How do you approach someone new about bringing toys into lovemaking?

22. If you don't, would you like to? Tell me what you would like to play with.

About Playing Pretend Games

1. Playing pretend can add spice to lovemaking. Have you ever done it? Played doctor? Pirate? Kidnapper or prison guard? Tell me about it.

2. If not, would you like to? What do you think would happen?

3. How would you react if your partner answered the door dressed like a police officer or a doctor?

About Your Fantasies

1. Do you fantasize while you make love? Describe any one (or more). How often do you fantasize? Have you told your partner?

2. Do you fantasize at other times? Describe one of those fantasies.

3. Do you fantasize about making love to another person? Who would it be?

4. Do you have a fantasy you haven't shared with your partner? Take some time and share it with me. Would you like to act it out, or should it remain just between us?

5. Do you dream about a threesome? With whom? Tell me all the delicious details.

6. Do you ever think about being watched while you're making love? Or watching another couple? Have you ever done it? How did (or would) the scene play out?

7. Have you ever fantasized about having sex in public?

8. Have you ever fantasized about being in control of, or being controlled by, your partner? How much control? Would you like to act it out? Have you ever? Describe.

9. Do you ever fantasize about pain being pleasure? How much?

10. Do you wish you could administer or receive the pain? Would you like to act it out? Have you ever? How would you like it to play out?

11. If you are straight, do you ever have homosexual fantasies? If gay, do you ever have heterosexual ones? Can you describe one?

And Lastly

The one thing I've never told anyone about my sex life is . . .